ITALIAN LINERS
OF THE 1960s
THE COSTANZI QUARTET

IAN SEBIRE

First published 2021

Amberley Publishing
The Hill, Stroud,
Gloucestershire, GL5 4EP

www.amberley-books.com

Copyright © Ian Sebire, 2021

The right of Ian Sebire to be identified as the Author
of this work has been asserted in accordance with the
Copyright, Designs and Patents Act 1988.

All rights reserved. No part of this book may be reprinted
or reproduced or utilised in any form or by any electronic,
mechanical or other means, now known or hereafter invented,
including photocopying and recording, or in any information
storage or retrieval system, without the permission in writing
from the Publishers.

ISBN: 978 1 3981 0806 6 (print)
ISBN: 978 1 3981 0807 3 (ebook)

British Library Cataloguing in Publication Data.
A catalogue record for this book is available from the British Library.

Typeset in 10pt on 13pt Celeste.
by SJmagic DESIGN SERVICES, India.
Printed in the UK.

Contents

	Preface	4
1	Nicolò Costanzi	5
2	*Galileo Galilei* and *Guglielmo Marconi*	11
3	*Oceanic*	50
4	*Eugenio C*	72
	Epilogue	93
	Acknowledgements	94
	Bibliography	95

Preface

Picture the scene. It is mid-morning on a peerless day in May 1965, out in the Gulf of Genoa a huge ocean liner lies serenely still, gleaming white under a cobalt sky, on a glassy smooth Mediterranean Sea. Superficially it is a picture of utter tranquility, however if we zoom in to a human scale it is clear something is amiss. Tension fills the air.

High up on the aft end of Promenade Deck a group of men are huddled in animated conversation, a circle of furrowed brows and anxious eyes. Despite their collective knowledge and experience they are perplexed by the liner's lack of pace and chronic vibration. In the centre stands a tall, somewhat portly septuagenarian, his wispy grey hair slightly ruffled, smoke drifts up from an inevitable cigarette. Moments later the elderly man clambers into a large rattan basket, which at his instruction crew members have placed and hopefully tied securely at the stern.

To those who witnessed them subsequent events must have seemed otherworldly. As *Michelangelo*'s mighty turbines rumble into life and the initial tremors manifest into intolerable rattling, the old man is lowered down until the basket is swaying precariously, just feet above the churning sea. There are no censors or clever camera aids, he simply watches and makes a mental picture, noting the nature and flow of the wash as the Italian flagship thunders along at close to 30 knots.

When I first read about the origins of the 'Costanzi cure' I assumed I must have translated it incorrectly. Having subsequently received eye-witness testimony I can vouch for its authenticity. What amazed me then and still does, almost above the courage, willingness to endure discomfort and sublime technical skill, was the sheer magnanimity of the man. We should remember that Costanzi's design for the new national flagships had been rejected (on political, rather than technical grounds) in favour of the Ansaldo tender. Yet here he was, having been drafted in by the exasperated experts of the rival Genoese shipyard and Italian Line technical teams, literally risking life and limb to find a solution to their quandary. Only he probably knows why he did it, but I suspect it is as much a testimony to his insatiable desire to resolve challenges, as it is to his professionalism or patriotism.

On his return to Trieste Costanzi instigated a number of adjustments to the sister ship's propellers and underwater configuration. The results allowed *Raffaello* to achieve a higher speed than her twin, with negligible vibration. The 'Costanzi cure' had achieved its purpose and was applied to *Michelangelo* later in the year. A dilemma had been resolved and a legend born.

1
Nicolò Costanzi

Those who achieve greatness in their chosen field invariably assume the mantle of genius. To the casual observer it's as if all the skills and knowledge required for such accomplishments are pre-programmed at birth, and therefore the end result both preordained and by association effortless. It's a title easily bestowed, however the wise know that undoubted natural ability and enthusiasm only go so far, greatness requires exceptional application as well as aptitude; in short 'genius' costs. In the field of ship design there have been a number of such men (and historically it has been a male preserve). Among the most prominent and yet enigmatic was Nicolò Costanzi, a man whose legacy continues to this day.

Costanzi was born as Nicolò Cossancig in his beloved Trieste (a city that changed nationality on seven occasions during his lifetime) on 19 October 1893. He was schooled at the local *K.K. Staats Gewerbeschule* until 1912, when his evident artistic talent led him to briefly study under the painter Guido Grimani. Despite retaining a passion for art and painting that would last the rest of his life he soon left to follow a different path.

Nicolò Costanzi: engineer, artist, genius. (Photographer/source unknown)

At the age of twenty-one Nicolò enrolled at the local *Scuola Superiore di Architettura Navale* and quickly stood out for his thoroughness and ingenuity. At this time (1914) Trieste was an autonomous city within the Austrian Littoral crown land, principal port and shipbuilding centre of the Austrian merchant fleet and the Austro-Hungarian Navy. In the late nineteenth and start of the twentieth century the city became renowned as a bustling conduit of the Habsburg empire, with grand architecture reflecting the best influences of Vienna, Budapest and Prague and world famous coffee houses frequented by a broad array of scientists, artists and philosophers. As the writer Jan Morris suggests 'This was an innovative, technological place, not hampered by nostalgia, and like the Chicagos and Manchesters it looked eagerly to the future'. The city was a cosmopolitan melting pot of ideas and influences for young Nicolò Cossancig.

Trieste was annexed by Italy at the end of the First World War. Cossancig initially served an apprenticeship with the technical department of the local San Marco and San Rocco di Muggia shipyards, but after qualifying in 1920 he was persuaded by the influential Cosulich family to join their technical team. He spent 1923 to 1924 in the UK, gaining experience and testing his already prodigious technical knowledge. British yards had been instrumental in building the Italian merchant fleet and at this time W Beardmore & Co Ltd,

The first of Costanzi's prolific output. *Saturnia* (seen here at her launch) and *Vulcania* were splendid examples of robust, beautiful vessels with excellent sea keeping qualities, characteristics with which their designer became synonymous. (Aldo Cavallini collection – naviearmatori)

based at Dalmuir on the banks of the Clyde, were constructing the last of a famous trio of Conte liners for Lloyd Sabaudo. Costanzi was being primed to work on a pair of new vessels for Cosulich Line's Trieste-New York service, which emerged as the distinctive and long-serving motor ships *Saturnia* and *Vulcania*.

By the age of thirty-two he was heading the technical department at Cosulich's nearby Monfalcone shipyard. The following year, 1926, as part of the 'Italianisation' policy implemented under Mussolini throughout the Julian March region, the young engineer's name was changed to Costanzi.

If *Vulcania* and *Saturnia* gave Costanzi a foothold, it was his next significant vessel which brought him to international prominence. Commissioned by Lloyd Triestino for their Eastern Mediterranean service, *Victoria* was rightly lauded as among the most beautiful and successful vessels yet conceived. Furthermore Costanzi's hull design is widely credited for the *Victoria*'s remarkable trials performance, in which she exceeded the projected maximum speed by almost two knots, thereby becoming the fastest motor liner afloat. Coupled with Gustavo Pulitzer Finali's 'Littorian' style interiors, the ship had an overall coherence that was both elegant and practical. Although initially operating on the Alexandria service, circumstance dictated that she subsequently sailed to the Far East, first to Bombay and ultimately Shanghai. Despite being only 13,000 grt *Victoria* caught the attention of the wider shipping fraternity and served as a template for a further, larger collaboration between the two men, the great transatlantic liner *Conte di Savoia*.

Two more important motor ships, *Neptunia* and *Oceania,* followed in the early 1930s which together with *Victoria* and *Conte di Savoia* engendered much valued overseas orders. Among the most prominent, paid for with coal shipments, were Polish Ocean Lines *Batory* and *Pilsudski*, while an even more exceptional barter arrangement (of dried cod, no less) paid for a pair of Bergen Line North Sea ferries. Perhaps the most significant CRDA order in this period was the unfulfilled *Stockholm* of 1938. Costanzi collaborated with Swedish America Line's renowned in-house designer, Eric Christiansson, to produce a dual-purpose liner and cruise ship that undoubtedly influenced his future thinking. Despite twice taking tangible form, first a shipyard fire and then destruction at the hands of allied bombers deprived the Swedes of their flagship.

Costanzi's skills were not limited to passenger ships. Among his prominent other work in the inter-war period was the battleship *Vittorio Veneto*. When Italy entered the war on the Axis side in 1940 he remained at Monfalcone and in 1943 was appointed director of CRDA. In this capacity he not only helped save the yard's facilities and equipment from destruction but also worked tirelessly to retain and maintain the morale and safety of the beleaguered workforce. Much more than an engineer, Costanzi was also a strong and influential character.

Despite the devastation wrought by the Second World War and its immediate aftermath, Costanzi's hard work and sheer weight of personality paid dividends. Having been passed from one occupying force to another (Italian, German, Yugoslav and the US and British respectively), some stability was finally restored when the Free Territory of Trieste was created under the auspices of the United Nations in 1947.

Situated on the cusp of the capitalist/communist ideological divide, Trieste and Monfalcone were under the protection and administration of the United States and British, for whom the city and its environs became a crucial strategic buttress. As one of the principal employers and industries in the region, shipbuilding, and CRDA in particular, received significant financial and material investment. The resurgence of post war Italian shipping started with the rebuilt *Conte Biancamano* and *Conte Grande*, quickly followed by the brand new *Augustus* and *Giuilio Cesare*. As the 1950s progressed Costanzi received lucrative offers from British, American and even Soviet shipyards but turned them all down to remain at CRDA.

Bridging the late 1950s and early 60s came the succession of orders covered by this book and which in many ways define the man and his craft. To these we can also add CRDA's concept for the new Italian Line flagships, which ultimately became *Michelangelo* and *Raffaello*. As alluded to in the preface, politics ultimately dictated that the Ansaldo shipyard's design was adopted, robbing the world of two of the most beautiful and intriguing vessels 'that never were'. Around this time Costanzi also developed and patented the unique bow and stern arrangements that to this day bear his name. In profile the bow, which was first seen with *Galileo Galilei*, featured a traditional concave curve near the waterline that turned into an atypical convex higher. Seen head on it provided an hourglass silhouette with the same concave/convex combination replicated below the waterline. In theory the design optimised water flow around the hull, improving fuel efficiency while also providing superb stability in all sea states. In practice the elegant prow achieved both these goals, effectively dispersing head seas while avoiding the slamming tendency associated with more conventional flared bows. The theory behind the hybrid stern is best described by another exceptional naval architect, Dr Stephen Payne:

> I have long believed that you have the best chance of success in an enterprise if you look back into history and appreciate earlier successes and failures. When I came to design *Queen Mary 2*, I faced a conundrum about the shape of the stern. Although *Queen Mary 2* definitely wasn't a cruise ship, she was to be a true liner, hydrodynamic considerations for powering favoured a cruise ship style transom stern. In some ways the shape of the underwater hull in the aft part of the ship almost mandated a transom stern, as four huge propulsion pods would be required to be mounted vertically in this region. However, sea keeping considerations pointed towards an elegant cruiser stern. The reason? On the North Atlantic and the large swells invariably encountered, even the largest and well-founded ship would pitch with the stern rising and falling as she progressed through the swells. With a vast transom stern and flat underbelly, the stern would crash into the swells causing considerable annoying noise and vibration, you can frequently experience this on cruise ships in port when the wash of passing ships causes the water surface to lap against the underside of the transoms.
>
> Remembering past adage, the solution was the 'Costanzi stern' developed by him for the *Oceanic* and *Eugenio C.* Both these fine ships had a hybrid transom/cruiser stern arrangement, presumably for the same reasons and I proposed such a stern for *Queen Mary 2*, minimising the transom element and maximising the cruiser form. Although initially sceptical, the French shipyard building *Queen Mary 2* model tested a hybrid stern, advising me that they would only agree to adopt it if it was proven to be beneficial -the shipyard was after all responsible for the as built speed performance of the ship. The resulting *Queen Mary 2* with the hybrid stern is testament that the concept works. The Costanzi stern lives on!

QM2's successful hybrid stern arrangement – Costanzi's principles applied to the twenty-first century. (Author's collection)

Esteemed by his peers, Costanzi won the gold award for the best design for the period 1957 to 1963 from the National Association of Engineers and Architects. Tage Wandborg, the renowned Danish naval architect perhaps most famous for the transformation of *France* into *Norway,* once commented;

> As a young man I regarded Nicolò Costanzi as my great hero. He not only revolutionised hull design and hydrodynamics through his rigorous research, but he was also an artist and a great aesthete. He was, in fact, a father figure and an architect whose sculptural methods, innovation and aesthetic judgement I admired.

Those he worked with often became personal friends, among them Pulitzer, Zoncado and Boica, a clear indication of both his warm personality and collaborative style. Although over seventy years old, there was to be one final significant passenger ship in the Costanzi repertoire after *Eugenio C,* the diminutive, bespoke cruise ship *Italia*, nicknamed the mini-*Oceanic*. His insatiably inquisitive mind continued working to the very end, not only devising the 'Costanzi cure' for *Michelangelo*'s woes but on new radical designs, including elaborate hydrofoil hulls.

Writing in 1976, Romano Boica recalled a tall, restless man, with sharp inquisitive eyes, 'always looking to the future'. Cigarettes were his principal vice, occasionally smoking two at a time! At once kind-hearted and irascible, Costanzi was also endearingly modest. Courage was clearly not an issue; any man who is prepared to be lowered in a rattan basket over the stern of a ship clearly has little problem in that regard.

Despite extensive research several aspects of Costanzi's personal life remain frustratingly elusive. For instance I cannot trace his parents, their occupations or influence over the young Nicolò. He lived in a house at Barcola, overlooking the shimmering Adriatic just north of Trieste (and a relatively short distance from CRDA's offices at Monfalcone), and I believe he was married with a family, although to whom and details of any offspring escape me. If anyone can enlighten me I would be most grateful. It is clear he never lost his love of painting and exhibited his beautifully atmospheric sea and landscapes throughout Italy.

When he died on 20 June 1967 the world lost an exceptional naval architect and a great man. Fortunately, this particular genius was also a generous and patient teacher, meaning his ideas and philosophy evolved through assistants like Fulvio Cernobori, who Stephen Payne proudly collaborated with at Fincantieri.

Passing the baton. Costanzi and a member of his team pour over blueprints. (Museo dela cantieristica Monfalcone collection)

2

Galileo Galilei and *Guglielmo Marconi*

The eighth of September 1960 was arguably the greatest day in the history of the Italian merchant marine. On that late summer Thursday, in a neatly choreographed publicity exercise, the keels of four great passenger liners were simultaneously laid on the stocks, representing the final element of the FINMARE group's investment in new tonnage. At the Ansaldo yard Genoa and Cantieri Riuniti dell'Adriatico's (CRDA) facility at Trieste, it was the genesis of the Italian Line's super-liners *Michelangelo* and *Raffaello*. Meanwhile, at CRDA's Monfalcone site, the first steel plates were ceremonially positioned for Lloyd Triestino's new flagships, yard numbers 1862 and 1863.

(Author's collection – www.sarniawatercolours.co.uk)

"GALILEO GALILEI"
27.500 Gross Tonnage - 26.4 knots - 702 ft. length - 94 ft. breadth fully air-conditioned, commissioned with her sistership "GUGLIELMO MARCONI" for the Italy/Australia Express Service.

An early artist impression of the new vessels. Note the simple funnel design. (Author's collection)

Unlike the ships whose conception date they shared, the Lloyd Triestino pair were ordered to meet clear market demands. Whereas the early twentieth century had been characterised by mass migration to the Americas, the post-war era lured many of Europe's poor, desperate and dreamers across the globe to Australia. With the promise of beautiful beaches, abundance (in the face of austerity back home) and a more egalitarian society, this new land of opportunity was heavily promoted by the Australian government, under their rather dramatically named 'populate or perish' policy. The key aims were to bolster the country's labour force and provide additional security against the regional influence of communist China.

One of the key inducements offered was the Assisted Passage Migration Scheme. Under this arrangement, the government subsidised the fares of emigrating Europeans, most

The beautifully svelte 702-foot-long hulls included an exceptionally slender entry at the waterline fore and aft, with pronounced tumblehome amidships. However it was the patented 'swan neck' bow that really caught the eye and became the trademark of Costanzi's prolific output in the 1960s. (Dante Flore collection)

famously coining the term 'ten pound poms' for British émigrés. Originally confined to Britons, the scheme was extended to other nationalities over subsequent years, including Italians from 1952. Lloyd Triestino were then operating the popular 12,000 grt motor ships *Australia*, *Oceania* and *Neptunia* but more capacity was needed to meet the rapidly increasing demand. Perhaps more significantly, in the late 1950s the rival P&O and Orient Lines ordered *Oriana* and *Canberra,* the largest and fastest liners on the run to date. These new vessels were to be Lloyd Triestino's riposte.

Neatly coordinating with Lloyd Triestino's 125th anniversary, yard number 1862 was named *Galileo Galilei* after the famous astronomer and polymath by Bianca Rosa Fanfani (wife of the incumbent Italian Prime Minister), before sliding into the waters of the Adriatic on 2 July 1961. These were the first Lloyd Triestino liners to break with the traditional company naming policy, eschewing the usual 'a' suffix (*Africa*, *Europa*, *Neptunia* etc) and adopting instead the Italian Line's preference for honouring famous national figures.

The new ships' profiles were particularly pleasing on the eye. As well as the patented bow, the stern had an equally harmonious spoon shape. The bridge sat a long way aft, behind cargo hatches and handling equipment and a protected First Class open promenade. Perhaps the superstructure looked less bulky than it was thanks to the height differential between the glass enclosed winter garden and the outdoor promenade on

Above left: The second vessel, hull 1863, was launched as *Guglielmo Marconi* on 24 September 1961. The ceremony was given extra poignancy when the great scientist/inventor's second wife Marquesa Maria Christina Marconi (seen here) consented to perform the naming ceremony. (Dante Flore collection)

Above right: Fitting out the sisters became a protracted process. It soon became apparent that building four large liners simultaneously was overstretching the country's raw material and labour resources, especially in the finishing trades. Here *Galileo Galilei* is framed by the stern of the soon to be launched *Oceanic*. (Eustachio Patalano collection – naviearmatori)

Above left: As with most liners, the crowning glory was undoubtedly the funnel. To amplify the airflow and catch errant smuts a sizable soot shield protruded from the lower casing. (Lloyd Triestino, Author's collection)

Above right: If the physics was interesting and the practical application successful, it was in the aesthetics department that the funnel was arguably most impressive. It simply looked good from every angle and complemented the rest of the profile perfectly. This photo is taken from the bridge wing as *Galileo Galilei* approaches Trieste to be opened to the public in March 1963. (Aldo Cavallini collection – naviearmatori)

Promenade deck. The lifeboats were accordingly stepped each side, with three forward (including a 'whaler') above the raised winter garden and the remaining six further aft above the promenade.

When it came to devising the stack, Professor Carlo Motarino of Turin Polytechnic suggested his radical and undeniably effective trellis funnel concept for the new Lloyd Triestino ships. Modified examples of this design would be adopted for the Italian Line's new flagships but Lloyd Triestino and the shipyard opted for an adapted, traditional shape instead. It was as if the slender, tapered casing had been sliced open and jacked up on a series of spindly stanchions. Theoretically, like the more extreme *Michelangelo/Raffaello* variant, this would create an updraft at the funnel's rear edge. The funnel's novelty factor (all ships of the era seemed to incorporate at least one) was a telescopic pipe extension that could be raised in low wind conditions, such as in port. Aft of the funnel the rear decks cascaded in a gentle, stepped arrangement, with the superstructure neatly contoured to mirror the tapering stern.

Accommodation was provided for a maximum of 1,668 passengers in two classes. Given the ship's principal emigrant service this was officially composed of just 154 in

First and 1,514 in Tourist, with cabins, public rooms and facilities arranged over nine passenger decks. There was an element of flexibility, with a number of interchangeable cabins allowing for an alternative arrangement of 289 First Class and 1,358 Tourist Class passengers. Like all new liners of that era the sisters were air-conditioned throughout, a necessity in the sweltering tropics.

The majority of public rooms for both classes were situated on *Ponte Passaggiata* – Promenade Deck, sandwiched by First Class cabins above and Tourist Class below. Looking down on them all were the most egalitarian 'passengers' on board; dogs, cats, birds and (remembering this was the 1960s and 70s!) monkeys occupied the most lofty accommodation, the 'one-class' kennels, situated within the deck house beneath the funnel on *Ponte Comando* – Bridge Deck.

At 2,960 ft² the First Class Lounge, farthest forward on Promenade Deck, was the largest room for the upper echelons of the passenger list. Flooring comprised acres of polished rubber linoleum, eminently practical given the ship's tropical route, if sometimes rather Spartan. Heading aft was the First Class drawing room, which could be readily combined for gala evenings and banquets, while the winter gardens on either flank provided a relaxing sheltered space to chat and gaze at the passing sea through floor to ceiling windows.

Above: The *Verbena* special First Class, two berth cabin, was situated forward on the starboard side of A deck. With double aspect windows to the side and forward it must have felt a very light and spacious room. (Lloyd Triestino, Author's collection)

Right: In contrast E-530 was a four berth tourist class cabin located near the waterline on E deck. It has a basin but no toilet or shower facilities which are located in a central block along the corridor. (Lloyd Triestino, Author's collection)

Galileo Galilei's First Class Lounge, featuring Pulitzer's décor with its side walls in veined macassar and all fittings, including the windows, of anodised gold. The fore and aft walls had a laminated plastic coating and included a polyester reproduction of her namesake astronomer's portrait. (Lloyd Triestino, Author's collection)

Romano Boica's First Class Lounge on *Guglielmo Marconi* reflected his and Costanzi's ethos that a ship's interiors should be harmonised with the external structural form. (Lloyd Triestino, Alberto Imparato collection)

The other main First Class rooms (except the restaurant), were the children's room on *Ponte Comando* and the Veranda on *Ponte Lido*. The Veranda incorporated a bar, dance floor and small grill room and opened directly onto the First Class Lido and swimming pool. With views out over the flanks and stern it was a favourite place to while away languid days, and with the ship's orchestra playing a varied programme of dance music, nights at sea.

Since they outnumbered their First Class shipmates tenfold it is unsurprising that the largest rooms on board were reserved for Tourist Class. The décor was subdued but functional, referred to in the *Syren and Shipping* as possessing 'a sober elegance' on *Galileo Galilei*. The linear lighting and vibrant fabric colours ran through both the ship's principal Tourist class rooms. The decorative theme of the Tourist Class drawing room (known as the *Sala Boboli*) on *Galileo Galilei* was historic Italian architecture, portrayed on the melamine clad transverse walls and in the silk curtains. Linking the drawing room and the main lounge further aft were the Zodiac (port side) and Astrolabe (to starboard) galleries, with displays of the constellations and astronomical equipment in honour of the ship's namesake. On *Guglielmo Marconi* the gallery featured early radio equipment.

Galileo Galilei's First Class interiors were the work of veteran designer Gustavo Finali Pulitzer, while the equivalent spaces on *Guglielmo Marconi* were entrusted to Romano Boico. An eclectic group including Aldo Cervi, Matteo Longoni and Umberto Nordio designed Tourist class public rooms.

Keeping the passengers pampered, fed and watered necessitated a huge logistical effort from the ship's company, officials ashore and their agents. Publicists revelled in the mind-boggling statistics; 175,000 eggs would be consumed on each twenty-three day voyage to Sydney, together with 46,000 kg of meat and poultry, accompanied by 45,000 kg of vegetables and 50,000 kg of fruit. The desalinisation plant could produce 320 tons of water per day for drinking, cleaning and cooling water.

In addition to the human cargo the ships provided 9,000 tons of freight capacity, comprising 182,729 cubic feet of general and 6,355 cubic feet of refrigerated space, in five separate holds. These were serviced by four 5-ton capacity cranes (two forward and two aft),

Covering 5,200 square feet *Galileo Galilei*'s *Sala Olimpia* was a spacious main lounge, located just aft of centre on *Ponte Passaggiata*. A spot to relax by day it became the main venue for entertainment, dancing and music for Tourist Class by night. This view is taken looking aft, showing the oval shaped walnut parquet dance floor. The chairs are also made from the same polished wood. (Lloyd Triestino, Alberto Imparato collection)

Guglielmo Marconi's equivalent *Sala Venezia*. Whether it's the intriguing hexagonal recessed light fixtures or the richly toned upholstery, it exudes a more sophisticated and luxuriant feel than her sister's *Sala Olimpia*. This view looks forward towards the band stand abutting the funnel exhaust casing. (G Boata collection – naviearmatori)

A postcard montage of exterior and interior Tourist Class space on *Galileo Galilei*. (Author's collection)

Behind the scenes an important innovation for the hard working laundry crew were these huge ironing machines, capable of flattening volumes of bed linen at the touch of a button. (Maurizio Gadda collection – naviearmatori)

For safety the firefighting equipment included a comprehensive automatic sprinkler system, a network of sea water fire hydrants and an alarm system linked to a signal panel located on the bridge. (Maurizio Gadda collection – naviearmatori)

Right: An interesting aerial perspective showing the forward holds and extensive cargo handling equipment together with the adjacent First Class glazed and shaded promenade area. Also visible at the foot of the forward bulkhead are the windows of the First Class Lounge. (Paul M. Creutz collection)

Below: *Galileo Galilei* finally departed Monfalcone on 20 March 1963, achieving a top speed of 26.77 knots in the course of speed trials off the Adriatic coast which allowed substantial reserves above her 24 knot service speed. (Maurizio Gadda collection)

four 5-ton and two 15-5 ton derricks attached to the forward kingposts. There were also two conveyor belts and a new Macgregor baggage handling system, which spanned the ship and extended through shell doors on each side when docked. With a 1 ton load capacity, this dramatically speeded up the disembarkation and embarkation process, particularly relevant in interim transit ports.

Galileo Galilei was gratefully, if belatedly, accepted by Lloyd Triestino on 23 March 1963. In the traditional manner for CRDA built vessels she visited Trieste and was opened up to the inquisitive public at the city's Maritime Station, just a short stroll from the imposing company headquarters at Piazza Unità d'Italia.

The usual mix of emotions filled the air on 22 April 1963 as *Galileo Galilei* embarked her first complement of passengers for Australia. Excitement was tinged with apprehension among the emigrants who made up the majority of her passenger complement. Final

Nursed by attendant tugs *Galileo Galilei* arrived at Genoa from Trieste for the first time. (Aldo Cavallini collection – naviearmatori)

Finally, sailing time arrived, lines were cast off and heralded by whistle salutes, *Galileo Galilei* inched away from the quay. High up, lining the decks, passengers waved feverishly to the hordes ashore amidst a sea of handkerchiefs and stifled tears. The languid nature of the ship's departure only fuelled the emotion charged atmosphere, as faces and features slowly melted away. (Paul M. Creutz collection)

farewells on the quayside were followed by a bustling eagerness to find the cabin, that transient home for the next three weeks. To help orientate them the company invested in clear and copious signage throughout the ship. Even in First Class, where the urbane and experienced predominated, a maiden sailing was a great leveler. The crew were novices too and would need time to orientate and adapt to their new ship.

On the bridge Captain Federico Caorsi and his officers vigilantly guided their new charge through the narrow confines of Genoa's inner harbour to the open sea. Having disembarked the pilot *Galileo Galilei* gathered pace towards her 24.5 knot service speed, while curious passengers explored her public rooms and amenities. A contemporary advertisement summarises the entertainment on offer: 'At sea, in port …. every night is Saturday night. Gay dances and nightclub parties, widescreen movies, horse racing, card parties, bingo and yes … even TV. There's so much good living and activity on board the big, white twins, you never have a chance to be bored!'

If it all sounds a little quaint and rudimentary by today's standards, *Galileo Galilei* and her sister were very popular ships. Whether sunbathing on the Lido, splashing in the pools or tucked on a deck chair along sheltered promenades, the daytime focus was definitely outdoors. Nevertheless card games in the eponymous room, or recitals, folk dancing demonstrations and dancing lessons in one of the ship's lounges proved popular and enduring pastimes. Many also took the opportunity to learn or improve their English, or attend one of the lectures arranged to inform emigrants about their new homeland.

Swimming pools and deck sports diverted the active, whilst adjacent lido areas provided ample sunbathing space. This view gazes down from *Ponte Comando* to the First Class Lido and pool on *Ponte Lido* and its Tourist Class equivalent a further two decks down on *Ponte Passaggiata*. (Lloyd Triestino, Author's collection)

The large expanse of screened teak decking on *Ponte Comando* (Captain's deck), included deck tennis, quoits courts and a couple of clay pigeon shooting platforms further aft on each flank. In this brochure image a group pose and relax near the base of the funnel, whilst in the background a (presumably unscripted) interloper walks in front of the First Class children's lido. (Lloyd Triestino, Author's collection)

Formal, spoon-fed distractions were limited by today's standards. Nevertheless if there was a greater emphasis on making your own entertainment this made the trip no less enjoyable. Many lasting friendships and memories were formed around the bars and lounges. (Lloyd Triestino, Author's collection)

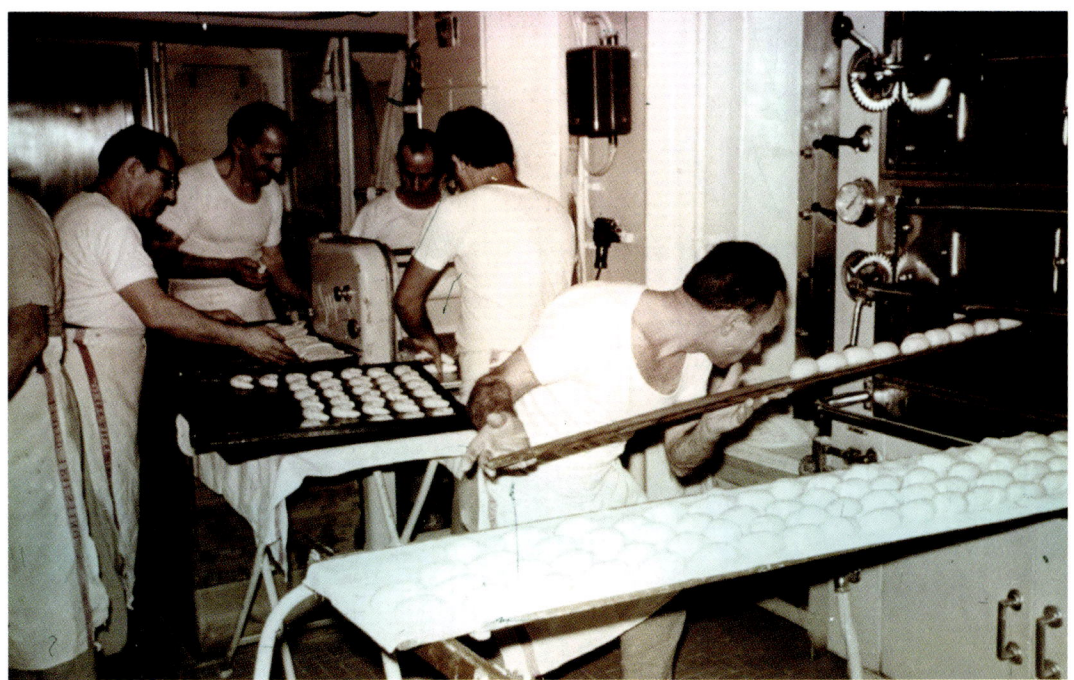

Ice cream maker Cesario Tosto (left) and Chief pastry chef Tommaso Cutugno (right) pose for the camera. (Maurizio Gadda collection – naviearmatori)

Bakers preparing a selection of rolls and pastries on board *Guglielmo Marconi*. (Maurizio Gadda collection – naviearmatori)

Meal times were eagerly anticipated and it's certainly true that dining on the sisters' rivalled anything served in the finest Italian restaurants afloat or ashore. (Lloyd Triestino, Author's collection)

Keeping children entertained for three weeks on a confined ship was no mean feat. However facilities were impressive and extensive including designated playrooms for each class, with everything from rocking horses and turntables to art equipment and books. (Lloyd Triestino, Author's collection)

Each class also had an outdoor Lido and paddling pool (here on *Guglielmo Marconi*), for children to enjoy. (Alberto Imparato collection)

From 'jelly and ice cream' parties to festive parades (here on *Galileo Galilei*), every effort was made to alleviate boredom for the little ones. (Lloyd Triestino, Author's collection)

Like other Italian lines Lloyd Triestino orchestrated mid-ocean rendezvous, allowing their passengers to enjoy the spectacle of two great ships passing improbably close, at a combined speed of 40-50 knots. Here *Galileo Galilei* is seen from fleet mate *Africa*. (Francesco Mistretta collection – naviearmatori)

Galileo Galilei moored at Aden. For more than a century this was a key bunkering post en route to the Orient. (Don Hazeldine collection)

Unlike the transatlantic sprint, the twenty-three-day passage to Sydney included several sightseeing stops and numerous languid days at sea. Those opting for tours of the pyramids and Cairo disembarked at Port Said, rejoining the liner at Port Suez after she had transited the canal. *Galileo Galilei* then steamed down the Red Sea to Aden. With the arid heat of Yemen behind her Lloyd Triestino's new flagship made for Bombay, where passengers with the means could opt for a variety of excursions, experiencing the intoxicating blend of sights, smells and sounds that were (and are) India. Doubtless enthralled but relieved to be back in their air-conditioned haven, they settled down to long days crossing the vast tracts of the Indian Ocean. Once they entered the Southern Hemisphere, the inertia aboard started to dissipate, replaced by a growing sense of anticipation. *Galileo Galilei* approached the Australian coast.

After calling at Fremantle *Galileo Galilei* rounded Point D'Entrecasteaux and crossed the Great Australian Bight, before discharging more emigrants turned immigrants at Melbourne's protruding Station Pier. From Melbourne she passed through the Bass Strait and bisected Sydney's sentinel Heads before docking at Circular Quay. It was journey's end.

Among the lengthening shadows of Autumn *Guglielmo Marconi* finally entered service, releasing *Neptunia* to join her sisters as Italia's Musicatti on the Central and South America service.

Periodic calls at Singapore notwithstanding, the voyage south east to Australia was punctuated by one other significant shipboard ritual. To the delight of voyeuristic onlookers, presided over by King Neptune and his henchmen in full regalia, a few unfortunate sacrificial transiting virgins were paraded, humiliated, daubed and ultimately dunked in the traditional 'crossing the line' ceremony. (Alberto Imparato collection)

First landfall on the new continent was Fremantle. A huge sign on the terminal building declared 'Welcome to Western Australia' for all those bound for 'Freo', Perth and their environs. (Author's collection)

With a backdrop of the iconic harbour bridge, *Guglielmo Marconi* is shown at Circular Quay, Sydney, following a twenty-three-day voyage from Genoa. (Aldo Cavallini collection – naviearmatori)

Work continues on fitting out *Guglielmo Marconi* at Monfalcone over the summer of 1963. (Maurizio Gadda collection – naviearmatori)

In the course of speed trials *Guglielmo Marconi* attained 26.83 knots, marginally higher than her sister. She was accepted by Lloyd Triestino on 30 October 1963 and entered service, five months late, in November 1963. (Aldo Cavallini collection – naviearmatori)

A picture of power and grace, *Guglielmo Marconi* at speed off the Liguria coastline. (Alberto Imparato collection)

The *Galileo* and *Marconi* subsequently maintained the Australia service with twelve annual round trips. Despite their delayed completion the Lloyd Triestino twins proved popular and successful in their new role. Although Italians predominated south bound, the passenger complement included a broad range of nationalities and calls at Piraeus drew a sizable Greek contingent. In addition to migrants Tourist Class was also the preserve of Australian students and twenty-somethings, venturing back and forth to Europe for holidays or work. Among the latter, anecdotes testify to the frequent romantic attraction between Italian junior officers and liberated young women, often enjoying their first trip away from parents and homeland.

In June 1967 Carmello Francesco Grasso was a seventeen-year-old on what would prove to be an historic *Guglielmo Marconi* voyage:

> We sailed from Messina to Piraeus to pick up some immigrants, and on towards Port Said on 4 June. However instead Captain Athos Pochintesta announced that we would be sailing past Suez, due to the eruption of the war in the area between Egypt and Israel. Therefore we continued towards Gibraltar, not stopping, but sighting it on our way to the Canary Islands, to Las Palmas for bunkering and supplies and then quite a few sea days till we arrived in Durban. We were in Durban for at least ten or twelve hours before departing for seven very rough seas days, until arriving in Fremantle, Western Australia. I think it was the 23rd or 24th of June 1967, where I disembarked early in the morning.

A busy scene at Piraeus, with *Guglielmo Marconi* in the process of docking and the last of Jadrolinija Line's three 2,500 ton 'J' class vessels, *Jedinstvo* in the foreground. (Mike Dale collection)

Captain Athos Pochintesta is a study of experience, concentration and quietly assured confidence on the bridge of the *Guglielmo Marconi*. A man seemingly at one with himself and the sea. (Maurizio Gadda collection – naviearmatori)

For the next eight years the ships were diverted via the Atlantic and Cape Town or Durban. Young South Africans now joined their Australian equivalents on migration to and from Europe.

Like thousands before them, in the late summer of 1967 the Tomarchio family made the momentous decision to leave their Sicilian home and travel half way around the world.

They were lured by the prospect of a new and rich life in Australia. Silvia Tomarchio recalls:

> My dad told a story of how people would say that there is money to be made and found everywhere, he said he saw money floating on the water on the way over.

Initially Silvia's father was due to travel alone. Primarily this was because his twenty-six-year-old wife was heavily pregnant with their fourth child. However in a late change of plan they purchased a family ticket, and the existing family members undertook the first leg of their journey to Genoa, where they boarded *Galileo Galilei* with just a few prized possessions. In fact Signora Tomarchio should not have mounted the gangway:
 'My mother told them that she was only six months pregnant or she would not have been allowed to board...'. She wasn't only defying the shipping company regulations; '... my grandma put a hex on her not to get on board, but she found whatever voodoo it was and burnt it'.
 Fifty two years on Silvia takes up the story:

> I used to be quite embarrassed by my parents, they would introduce me as the one born on a ship, or their friends would say "oh this is the one born on the way", but now I realise what a privilege and how unique it is. My passport has "At sea" as place

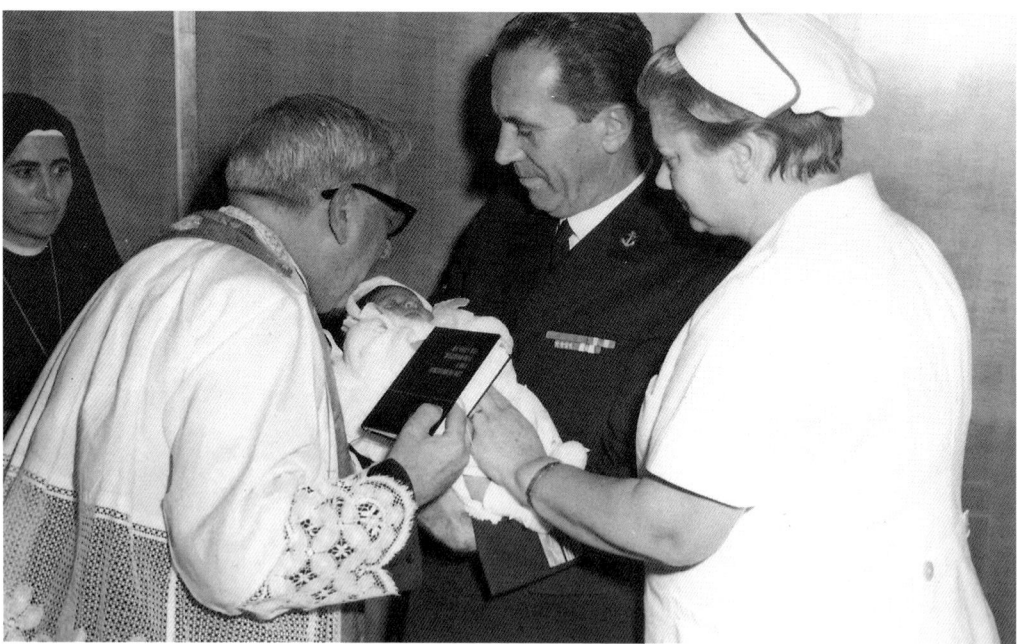

Nineteen days earlier than expected, as the Lloyd Triestino flagship skirted the African coast off Liberia, Mrs Tomarchio gave birth to a baby girl. The new member of the Tomarchio family was christened a week later, as *Galileo Galilei* approached Durban. She was named Silvia Lidia, after her Godfather Captain Rudolfo Sangulin's (centre holding the baby) wife, and the ship's nurse (right) who delivered her. (Silvia Tomarchio collection)

of birth, which has always made for interesting conversation when I travel. My dad took a photo of a witch doctor in Durban. For the first eleven years of my life my brother made me believe he was my real dad, and I carried it in my wallet! Brothers!

When the Tomarchio family disembarked in Melbourne a journey had ended but it was the start of a whole new adventure.

My parents, three siblings and I initially stayed with a family, then they rented and by the time I was about four they purchased our first family home. They still live there but when I was eleven they knocked it down and built a new house.

Silvia's tale seems remarkable, but it isn't unique. She was in touch with another Silvia (Novak), born and christened in identical circumstances six months earlier. Once again Captain Sangulin took on the role of godfather and the baby took his wife's first name. Both women tried to track down their godfather and namesake in Trieste. Silvia Tomarchio recalls:

I managed to speak to the captain and he knew exactly who I was. He was really happy that I called but by my second call he had passed away and I spoke to his wife Silvia, also lovely. In 1988 I went to Trieste to find them, although whoever answered said they were away, gutted! I was at their door and never got to meet them.

While the impact of air travel was initially less conspicuous than on the Atlantic, competition from other shipping lines was intense. In addition to P&O and Orient Line, fellow Italians Cogedar, Sitmar and Star Lauro introduced newly renovated vessels in the early to mid-1960s. Arguably the greatest threat to the Lloyd Triestino twins came from a relative newcomer to the trade, the Greek Chandris Line. When Chandris secured the Assisted Passage contract and Lloyd Triestino's market share dwindled, they responded by introducing an around-the-world service.

On 4 January 1968, the *Marconi* inaugurated the around-the-world itinerary, out to Sydney via Cape Town but then on to Brisbane, Suva (Fiji), Pago Pago (American Samoa), Acapulco, Balboa and the Panama Canal. She then called at Colón, Kingston and Port Everglades, before crossing the Atlantic to Madeira and Lisbon, arriving at Genoa two months and five days after leaving. (Lloyd Triestino, Author's collection)

Following her sister's lead, on 3 August 1968 *Galileo Galilei* departed Genoa for her first circumnavigation, thereafter alternating the extended itinerary with the conventional liner service. From June 1971, she was assigned to around the world voyages full time, with a slightly amended itinerary including calls at New Zealand, New Caledonia, Papete in Tahiti, Acapulco, Willemstad (Curacao) and Malaga before Messina, Naples and Genoa. *Guglielmo Marconi* joined her sister on this year-round service in 1972. The new schedule proved popular, attracting a mix of point-to-point and tourist traffic and supplemented by occasional cruises, in particular from Sydney to New Zealand and the South Pacific.

Alberto Imparato's wonderful rendition of the meeting of *Guglielmo Marconi* and *Leonardo da Vinci* on Gatun Lake, Panama Canal in March 1970. The former was on one of her circumnavigations, the latter on her one and only foray to the Pacific. (Alberto Imparato collection)

Approaching a lock on the Panama Canal – note the deckhands on the forward mooring deck preparing to throw a line to one of the locomotives, affectionately known as mules, which will help guide and pull the ship through the lock. (Lloyd Triestino, Author's collection)

Guglielmo Marconi rests between voyages at Genoa. Soon such scenes would be confined to history (itsfoto)

Like much of the world's merchant fleet, by the early 1970s Lloyd Triestino's worldwide passenger network entered a period of terminal decline. Spiralling fuel costs, intransigent, militant unions and inflexible management created a toxic cocktail at a time when revenues were shrinking. The result was perhaps inevitable. On 25 March 1975, the Minister for the Merchant Marine announced that FINMARE's long-distance services would be phased out by the end of 1977. As if anticipating the worst, *Galileo Galilei* hit on uncharted reef off the African coast on her first outbound voyage that year. After an inspection at Monrovia revealed considerable hull damage she was forced to return to Genoa on 24 January 1975 for permanent repairs. As part of its obligations under the retrenchment programme, Lloyd Triestino transferred *Guglielmo Marconi* to the Italian Line's South America service on the penultimate day of 1975, as a replacement for *Augustus*.

Claudio Savino was one of two Italian Line officers assigned to ensure a smooth transition for her new role:

> We were sent to Acapulco in December 1975, the *GM* was on her last voyage back from Australia to Genoa. The ship was well managed, better on the technical and passenger side than *Raffaello* and *Michelangelo*. The Italian Line took over full responsibility on 2 January 1976 after a total change of crew and staff. As you can imagine the takeover period was not an easy phase and I spent New Year's Eve on board with very little sleep. Anyway it all went well and I remained on board for the next six months. It was an interesting trade and on the personal front I met my wife on *Guglielmo Marconi*.

Galileo Galilei maintained the Australian run single-handedly into 1976, although strikes by disillusioned crew members continued to disrupt the schedules, which were planned through to December. With morale plummeting discipline on board also started to collapse, apathy frequently displaced customer service. The fact that Lloyd Triestino crews had been such an integral part of the ships' appeal only made the subsequent deterioration worse and while the camaraderie lingered it began to be tainted. Perhaps the worst example

Above: After little more than a change of funnel livery *Guglielmo Marconi* cast off from Naples on 18 January 1976. This was Italia's final maiden voyage, terminating in Buenos Aires on 4 February. (Italian Line, Alberto Imparato collection)

Left: The high life on the high seas. Italian Line publicity for *Guglielmo Marconi* was squarely aimed at a young, more informal demographic. (Italian Line, Alberto Imparato collection)

of that shipboard malaise came with the infamous Acapulco 'mutiny' of 1976. Josephine Cicio recalls, 'I remember that we were asked to stay in our cabins. I was only thirteen and I thought looters from the port were on our ship.' Crew member Alfredo Salomoni also witnessed those events:

> I was on board. Bad times. Guests, rioters, were not conscious of what they were doing. We arrived late in Acapulco after receiving an SOS from a Japanese vessel with a badly injured crew member on board. We had to change course and lowered one of our rescue boats with a medical team. The entire operation took a long time and we sailed to Acapulco at full speed but arrived very late, shortening the stay. The rioters were all arrested by Mexican Police ..... This is the history, almost.

Perhaps it's just a matter of translation or maybe that 'almost' speaks volumes.

In fact both vessels and their crews were soon put out of their misery. *Galileo Galilei* was alongside at Genoa, preparing for her 26 May 1977 sailing to Australia, when an impromptu announcement cancelled the voyage. One hundred and forty-two years of history was suddenly, dispassionately terminated as Lloyd Triestino's passenger services came to an abrupt end. In the South Atlantic a similar dislocation was being effected. On 21 May *Guglielmo Marconi* slipped her lines at Buenos Aires, edged into the River Plate and commenced her last crossing to Naples. Arriving on 7 June, she was laid up alongside her sister at Genoa.

The Italian government, in the guise of FINMARE, was now stuck with a still young yet commercially anachronistic fleet. With an eye to the expanding North American cruise industry, they came to an arrangement with several privately owned shipping lines

Although thanks to industrial action his family's voyage back from Italy to Australia took six weeks rather than the scheduled four, Dennis Kenna was inspired to create this magnificent scratch-built model of *Galileo Galilei*. (Dennis Kenna collection)

On 21 October 1977, *Galileo Galilei* arrived at the Cantieri Navali Riuniti shipyard, Palermo and is shown in the yard's dry dock beginning her conversion into a 900 berth cruise ship. (Aldo Cavallini collection – naviearmatori)

(most notably Costa and Flotta Lauro) to establish Italia Crosiere Internazionale (ICI). The basic premise was simple, the government would fund the conversion of the *Galileo, Marconi* and more modest refits for *Leonardo da Vinci* and Adriatica's *Ausonia*, while the private companies would bring a commercially viable management and business model. Alas it was a consortium founded on mistrust. Flotta Lauro withdrew early in the negotiations, their stake acquired by Maglivers, operators of the Trans Tirreno Express ferry service.

Much hung on the performance of *Guglielmo Marconi* which would operate year round from New York in direct competition with established cruise ships, notably Home Lines *Oceanic*. In a predictable case of déjà vu the conversions and fitting out of both sisters became inordinately protracted and costly. Once again shipyard strikes and material shortages were to blame.

On a bright sunny morning the *Marconi* arrived in New York from her Neapolitan refit, mobbed by helicopters, flanked by tugs and celebratory fireboat spray, it superficially looked like a return to halcyon days.

Marc Lewis recalls:

I did visit the *Marconi* when she was operated by ICI and first came to New York in December 1978. Greatly missing the ships of the Italian Line, I so very much WANTED to like her but something was missing. While very clean and well-maintained her interiors were tired and dated. She seemed like the poor, country cousin of *Raffaello* and *Michelangelo*; even to *Leonardo Da Vinci*. I guess I could best compare her interiors to *Da Vinci*'s Cabin Class at best and to her Tourist Class at worst. In addition, and in such contrast to all the Italian-crewed ships I had been on, at an intangible level, she lacked spirit. Even just to the visitor, that happy, warm and exuberant atmosphere customarily found the minute you stepped aboard an Italian ship, was simply not there. I left her that day thinking she will not succeed in the North American market, or certainly not the New York market where people expected a top draw, first class operation, comparable to Home Lines, Chandris or Flagship Cruises. She lasted months.

The sister's only significant external modification when operating for ICI was the removal of the forward kingposts. If anything they looked even smarter. Internally the existing First Class berths were supplemented by an additional 387 en suite cabins, some of which were installed in the former First Class dining room. (Bill Miller collection)

Although *Guglielmo Marconi*'s maiden 18 December 1978 Christmas cruise had been cancelled due to refurbishment delays, a subsequent ten day New Year cruise to St Thomas, San Juan and Martinique sailed with a 90 per cent load factor. Advanced bookings provided cause for optimism. On 27 March 1979, *Galileo Galilei* left Palermo for Genoa and commenced a series of Western Mediterranean cruises. The first of these departed on 11 April calling at Barcelona, Casablanca, Las Palmas and Lisbon.

The initial optimism was brutally quashed. In July 1979 press reports were released, on the direction of New York State Attorney General Robert Abrams, stating that *Guglielmo Marconi* had failed a health inspection, specifically that her galley equipment and water chlorination system did not meet current US legislation. The $8 million refit had clearly not addressed these basic requirements. After further inspection failures ICI decided to withdraw her from service, cancelling all subsequent ex-New York cruises on 10 August 1979.

Galileo Galilei was due to cross the Atlantic at the end of her summer European season to take up a series of cruises out of Port Everglades. Fearful, or simply resigned to the fact that she too would fail the inspection regime, ICI opted instead to give *Guglielmo Marconi* a comprehensive overhaul before taking up her sister's Caribbean itinerary. With no alternative employment planned *Galileo Galilei* was laid up at Genoa on 19 September 1979. The *Marconi* left Port Everglades on 20 October 1979 for her first winter season cruise but another failed inspection proved fatal. The press revelled in the once great ship's downfall, embellishing and sensationalising her apparent flaws. Further modifications costing $1 million in December 1979 did little to redeem a reputation in tatters. Without ceremony on the morning of 12 January 1980, *Guglielmo Marconi* arrived back at Port Everglades under the watchful gaze of Captain Giovanni Luigi Cortassa, after a weeklong cruise to San Juan, St Thomas and St Martin. The 502 passengers hastily disembarked, perhaps ignorant of the fact they were part of history as the final passengers to be carried on an Italian Line vessel. Initially she was moved to a spare berth at Port Canaveral but in September crossed the Atlantic and joined her sister, tethered in lay-up at Genoa Sestri. *Guglielmo Marconi*'s hibernation would last three long years but initially at least *Galileo Galilei* was more fortunate.

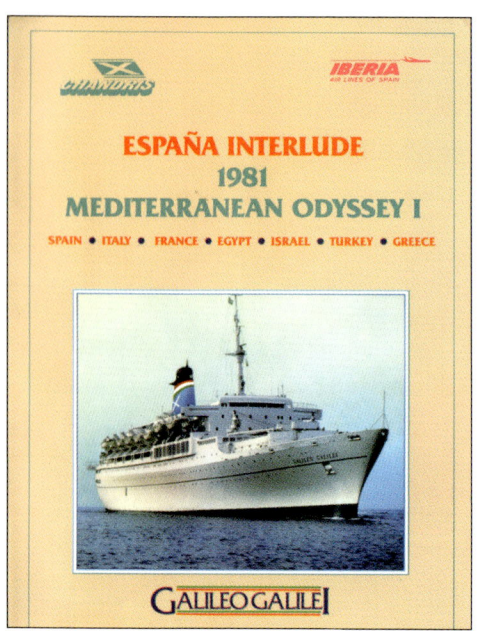

Left: A brochure for Chandris' 1981 'Mediterranean Civilisations' cruise programme. (Don Leavitt collection)

Below: Sporting Costa funnel colours but with her name painted out, a tired looking *Guglielmo Marconi* awaits her transformation into *Costa Riviera* at Genoa. (Aldo Cavallini collection – naviearmatori)

Chandris, Lloyd Triestino's nemesis on the Australia service was at this time looking to expand its operations in the newly resurgent Mediterranean cruise market. With this in mind *Galileo Galilei* was chartered for a series of fourteen night Mediterranean cruises from Genoa between 6 June 1981 and 24 October 1981. The punishing schedule included calls at Cannes, Barcelona, Syracuse, Alexandria, Haifa, Izmir, Piraeus and Naples before returning to Genoa. So satisfied were Chandris with the success of these voyages (the *Galileo* was faster and more fuel efficient than the previous incumbent, *Ellenis*)

that they planned an even more extensive 1982 programme. This included cruises from Amsterdam to the fjords and Baltic capitals, as well as ex-Genoa cruises to the Atlantic Islands. Unfortunately, when negotiations collapsed the ship returned to Genoa to join her sister in lay-up. They remained pathetically impotent, deteriorating in a corner of the Italcantieri yard throughout 1982 and well into 1983.

With no further employment having materialised, in the summer of 1983 the ships were offered for sale by the Italian Government.

Costa Line bid for both vessels, however Chandris made an offer on *Galileo Galilei* which they had operated so successfully in 1981, buying her for US$4 million through a Panamanian subsidiary. Costa meanwhile took ownership of *Guglielmo Marconi*, which having been inactive for three-and-a-half years was in a dilapidated state. Contracts for both ships were signed on 22 October 1983 and the respective owners immediately sent them to Genoese shipyards for modification and modernisation.

Renamed *Galileo*, Chandris' new acquisition completed her $10 million renovation in May 1984. The increased capacity of 1,262 passengers utilised the original public rooms augmented by a health club in place of the children's room and a casino supplanting one of the original lounges. As an indication of changing times the Veranda Bar became the Disco Club and the new Fantasy Lounge was formed by amalgamating the former First Class main lounge and ballroom.

Galileo's first employment was to sail to Bermuda. While her destination remained constant, her home port was not and in a nomadic summer she offered trips departing from a broad range of East Coast ports, from Boston to Charleston. In the autumn she headed south to Miami, offering short cruises over the winter 'low season', through until the following spring.

Chartered to Fantasy Cruises, *Galileo* generally retained her original silhouette, including the elegant funnel. The most conspicuous external modification was the extension of the forward superstructure on Amalfi and Promenade decks, to create 59 new cabins (32 of which were outside with large picture windows). (Paul M. Creutz collection)

Above: The aft deck cranes were also removed, the Lido decks extended and a new bar installed. Compare the models' awkward grins to the earlier 'snapshot' Lloyd Triestino brochure images and the smoothly polished Celebrity publicity material that follows. (Marc Lewis collection)

Left: In May 1985 *Galileo* was back sailing out of New York, before recommencing her nomadic role from the previous year. Again these were mainly to Bermuda but there was some variation, with cruises as far north as Halifax, and south to Nassau. She also offered the ubiquitous one night 'cruises to nowhere'. (Marc Lewis collection)

Redesigned by noted Danish naval architects Knud E Hansen A/S, little of the original external incarnation remained when *Guglielmo Marconi* emerged from the Mariotti yard as the totally transformed *Costa Riviera*. At $50 million Costa had invested five times as much as Chandris but in return they received, in effect, a brand new ship. (Paul M. Creutz collection)

The internal transformation was equally dramatic. The threadbare remnants of the *Marconi* were transformed into a sophisticated cruise ship of the 1980s by Giuseppe De Jorio. (Marc Lewis collection)

Costa used every cliché available to get over the message that *Costa Riviera* provided 'Cruising Italian Style'. (Marc Lewis collection)

On 23 November 1985 *Costa Riviera* left Genoa with travel agents and the media on board for an introductory mini cruise along the Ligurian coast. Four days later she left Italy and sailed at a sedate 17 knots, utilising her de-rated turbines, to Fort Lauderdale. While a number of stalwarts remained, *Costa Riviera* became the fulcrum around which the company fleet underwent a total transformation, symbolically she was the first Costa Line vessel not to be named after a family member. So pleased were they with the result that Costa subsequently commissioned the Mariotti yard to undertake an even more ambitious project, transforming a pair of container ships into the cruise ships *Costa Marina* and *Costa Allegra* that entered service at the end of the decade.

In mid-December *Costa Riviera* embarked her first fare paying passengers and left Fort Lauderdale on a maiden Caribbean cruise. (Marc Lewis collection)

44

Over the next few years both *Galileo* and *Costa Riviera* settled in to a seasonal cruising pattern, autumn through to spring in the Caribbean, with summers in Alaska (Costa Riviera) and Bermuda/US East Coast (*Galileo*). In October 1985 Chandris bought out Fantasy Cruises and for 1986 *Galileo* received a substantial refit, including new carpets and soft furnishings for the majority of cabins and public rooms. The following year she was involved in an extraordinary incident on one of her many visits to Bermuda. As night fell on Thursday 24 September 1987 *Galileo* was anchored in the Great Sound, her deep draught precluded her tying up in Hamilton. The Bermudan authorities advised that Hurricane Emily would pass over the island the following afternoon, so as a precaution the Captain announced an earlier Friday morning departure, the intention was to ride out the storm in the relative safety of the open sea. As it transpired Emily proved notoriously unpredictable, accelerating and veering towards the island, thereby trapping *Galileo*. With her bow to the wind and anchors straining the Chandris ship was soon riding 20-foot waves, her engines at full ahead just to maintain her position away from the nearby shoreline. When a sailor was swept into the sea from his foundering yacht and drifted towards the *Galileo*, crew members heroically lowered a lifeboat and plucked the bedraggled victim to safety. Emily tore through Bermuda, unleashing an unprecedented trail of destruction but by Saturday the storm had subsided sufficiently for *Galileo* to leave and set course for New York.

With the exception of *Galileo* the Chandris fleet at this time consisted of a variety of rebuilt British and American liners. All were beloved, in part for their quirky 'vintage' feel but it was evident that to progress in the increasingly competitive market the company would need to invest in new, more efficient tonnage. Various second-hand options were considered but ultimately the board decided to order a brand new vessel in April 1988.

Despite the untimely death of its founder Anthony Chandris in November 1984, his eponymous cruise line continued to flourish as the decade progressed, under the guidance of his debonair, cultured son John. *Galileo* spearheaded the company's growth and utilised a new deep water berth, at Kings Wharf, to avoid tendering complications at Bermuda. (Paul M. Creutz collection)

At 45,000 tons the $185 million state of the art cruise ship was considerably larger than her fleet mates and pencilled in to replace *Amerikanis*. In fact the vessel, named *Horizon*, would enter service for a new subsidiary called Celebrity Cruises.

Celebrity emerged from the need to meet specific requirements dictated by the Bermuda Government. It was at once a gamble and an inspired move, ultimately spawning one of the most successful cruise lines of the modern era. In April 1988 Home Lines was acquired by Holland America Line (HAL) and the new owners gave notice of their intention to withdraw from the Bermuda trade. Chandris was keen to exploit the resulting void which provided preferential berthing rights at Hamilton, as well as exclusive sailings in the high summer season. In the same month that Home Lines was purchased by HAL and the contract for *Horizon* was signed, Celebrity Cruises was formed. The Bermudan contract required two vessels to provide weekly sailings between May and October, *Horizon* would be completed just in time but none of Chandris' existing tonnage could meet the expected standard. The solution was to transform *Galileo* into a high-class contemporary cruise ship. In October 1989, having completed her summer cruise programme, *Galileo* crossed the Atlantic and entered the Lloyd Werft yard on the banks of the Wesser, to commence her transformation. To reduce costs Chandris continued its earlier practice by supplying 500 of its own employees to supplement the German workforce.

Already delayed by over-running work *Meridian*'s delivery voyage to Port Everglades was a torrid affair. She left Bremerhaven on 1 March 1990 and endured a succession of Atlantic storms, resulting in damage to the bow and a propeller which necessitated an unscheduled dry-docking at the Newport News dockyard. Having cancelled the first two

After four months and $55 million dollars the former *Galileo* emerged as the rechristened *Meridian*. She now resembled her erstwhile sister *Costa Riviera*, primarily due to the extension of the aft superstructure. Nevertheless retention of the original mast and a less modified funnel meant she kept something of her original elegance. (Paul M. Creutz collection)

Above left: *Meridian*'s Zodiac club. Internally, the prolific Athens based husband and wife team of Agni and Michalis Katsourinis (AMK Architects & Design) created a spacious, lavish, light and sophisticated feel. (Author's collection)

Above right: 'I'll have whatever she's having'. By the 1990s all cruise line brochures featured passengers, i.e. models, in various states of rapture. Celebrity had tapped into a niche market of young professionals who appreciated their ships' spacious interiors, sophisticated dining (which uniquely for the time included menus devised by celebrity chef Michel Roux), extensive fitness and spa facilities and lavish art collections. (Marc Lewis collection)

cruises, her initial voyage with fare paying passengers left Port Everglades on 1 April 1990, for Antigua, St Thomas and Nassau. Later in the month she made her first trip to Bermuda, subsequently sailing there from various East Coast ports but predominantly New York. At the end of October, she repositioned to Port Everglades for a Caribbean cruise programme. With the exception of occasional ventures to South America and the South Pacific this perennial cycle continued for the rest of her seven year Celebrity career, during which she remained a profitable and popular ship.

Costa Riviera proved similarly successful and spawned an influx of new tonnage, so that by the early 1990s Costa were considering new roles for their older ships. In 1993 they formed a joint venture company with Bruce Nierenberg, an influential American shipping entrepreneur and founder of Premier Cruise Lines. Both *Eugenio Costa* and *Costa Riviera* were earmarked for America Family Cruises but ultimately it was only the latter that was reassigned.

In September 1993 *Costa Riviera* entered the INMA shipyard at La Spezia for a US$25 million refit. An entire deck of public rooms was gutted and refurbished expressly for children. Cabins were adapted with more upper berths installed, substantially increasing capacity from 974 to 1,500 for the new family orientated venture. (Alberto Imparato collection)

On 18 December the officially renamed *American Adventure* left Fort Lauderdale on a maiden cruise to the Caribbean.

The experiment failed. Within a year American Family Cruises ceased trading and *American Adventure* returned to Genoa, reverting to *Costa Riviera*. Over the next seven years she was primarily based in the Mediterranean, ultimately though she started to show her age. Plumbing problems were among the most prominent of the old ship's woes and on 16 February 2002 it was announced that the almost forty-year-old vessel had been sold to Alang breakers for $1.7 million. Renamed *Liberty* she arrived off the Gujarat Coast on 7 March 2002, was run ashore and dismantled. By then however her sister had met an even more dramatic end.

As the oldest and smallest unit of the fleet, *Meridian*'s days were assuredly numbered when Royal Caribbean secured ownership of Celebrity in July 1997. Just two months after the acquisition, on 26 September 1997, *Meridian* departed Bermuda's Kings Wharf for the final time, arriving at Baltimore two days later. She had been purchased by Singapore based Sun Cruises for a reputed US$65 million. Desecration, both literal (the chapel was removed) and metaphorical is the most appropriate term for the ensuing transformation. Several public rooms including the Cinema and Zodiac club were stripped bare and casinos and gaming tables installed. Cabins at the forward end of Atlantic deck were eliminated to make way for a further VIP casino, while the Four Seasons Restaurant was converted into a buffet.

On 1 October 1997 the renamed *Sun Vista* crossed the Atlantic and made her way to Piraeus, where additional materials were taken on board and debris removed. She then sailed to Singapore for completion of the refit at the Sembourang Shipyard.

The alternating five (including calls at Binton, Tiomar, Malacca, Penang and Medonand) and two night itineraries met with short-lived success. Within a year bookings dwindled and by early May 1999 it was reported that Premier Cruise Line, the great champion of superannuated liners, was interested in buying her. They never got that chance.

On the afternoon of Thursday 20 May 1999, at around 14:30, *Sun Vista* was steaming through the Strait of Malacca, completing the final leg of a five-night trip, when a switchboard that was under repair short-circuited, sparking a fire. Passengers were notified that there was a 'minor incident' in the engine room and invited on deck for a barbeque. To allay fears and presumably keep them happy, an open bar was also enacted. Meanwhile the engine room crew tried valiantly but unsuccessfully to contain the blaze. Along the ships corridors lights were extinguished, the engines went quiet and smoke swirled aloft from the funnel casing. The ship started to drift. As the air-conditioning system failed passengers venturing below decks reported smoke filled passageways and cabins. At 18:30, with flames now engulfing the funnel casing, the Captain belatedly sent out a distress signal and passengers were called to their muster stations before being ordered into the boats. Chaos ensued.

For a time the crew continued to douse the flames but accumulating water from an attendant firefighting tug created a progressive list, so ultimately they too abandoned the vessel. Conditions were calm but nevertheless passengers and crew spent an uncomfortable six hours drifting in the busy sea lanes before being rescued by a container ship and units of the Malaysian Navy. In the early hours of the following day, the lonely, abandoned former *Galileo Galilei* paused, rolled on her side and descended to the seabed sixty metres below.

Externally the only obvious alteration was a change of funnel livery but inside Sun Vista was ready for a very different clientele. Sun Cruises business model was based on taking significant revenue from the gambling tables, one of the most appealing pursuits to their target Asian market. (Author's collection)

Fortunately it was low season, with barely a third of capacity on board. Amidst screaming children and fainting geriatrics the lifeboats were swung out, life rafts launched and all 472 passengers were ordered to abandon ship. (Author's collection)

3

Oceanic

Pinpointing the transition from traditional liner services to the subsequent cruise industry is an elusive task. Nevertheless waypoints exist, significant ships and events that in hindsight are indicative of a sea change. *Oceanic* was one such vessel.

She was ordered by Home Lines, a cosmopolitan alliance of Swedish American Line, the Cosulich family and Greek tycoon Eugen Eugenides, which initially provided berths for the burgeoning emigrant trade from Southern Europe to South America, at the end of the Second World War. The Swedes were particularly influential, providing the name (Home was an

(www.sarniawatercolours.co.uk)

anglicised version of the Swedish *holm*), livery (the distinction being the blue disc on the yellow funnel contained just a single crown rather than Swedish America's three) and two of the original three liners. Initial success ended abruptly in 1949 as the collapse of the Argentine currency and economy dried up the flow of migrants. The trio were initially diverted to a Mediterranean–New York route before forging a lucrative service from Northern Europe to Canada. By the late 1950s plans were being devised for the company's first new ship.

The proposed 1,600 berth vessel would have revolutionised the St Lawrence service, then dominated by Cunard and Canadian Pacific, coupling exceptional speed with space and facilities unheard of since *Empress of Britain* in the 1930s. At 39,000 tons the new ship was to be 10,000 tons larger than her rivals and like that famous pre-war liner she would double as a luxury, off season cruise ship. In 1960 Home Lines placed an order with CRDA.

The 782-foot-long hull has been justifiably lauded as one of the most efficient ever. In addition to Costanzi's trademark 'swan neck' bow it also incorporated his recently developed hybrid stern for the first time. Another notable feature was the absence of sheer. The ship was clearly designed with the rigours of the North Atlantic in mind, evidenced by a long fo'c'sle and a prominent breakwater.

In the summer of 1963 the Home Lines board met to discuss a radical proposal. Rather than plying between Europe and Canada it was proposed that the new ship should be placed on a year-round cruise service from New York to Nassau in the Bahamas.

While certainly bold, Home Lines were actually making a well-reasoned decision. With aircraft securing an escalating proportion of North Atlantic passenger traffic they correctly predicted a rapid decline for the shipping alternative. In 1960 *Italia* was refitted and experimentally switched to a year-round New York-Nassau cruise role, the only variation being longer Caribbean schedules in mid-winter. Her success prompted the company to reappraise their entire transatlantic involvement. Although *Homeric* remained on the service to Quebec and Montreal until 1963 she was destined to take over from *Italia* the

The first flag-bedecked keel segment of yard number 1876, Home Lines new flagship, is laid in place on the slipway at Monfalcone, 29 October 1961. (Aldo Cavallini collection – naviearmatori)

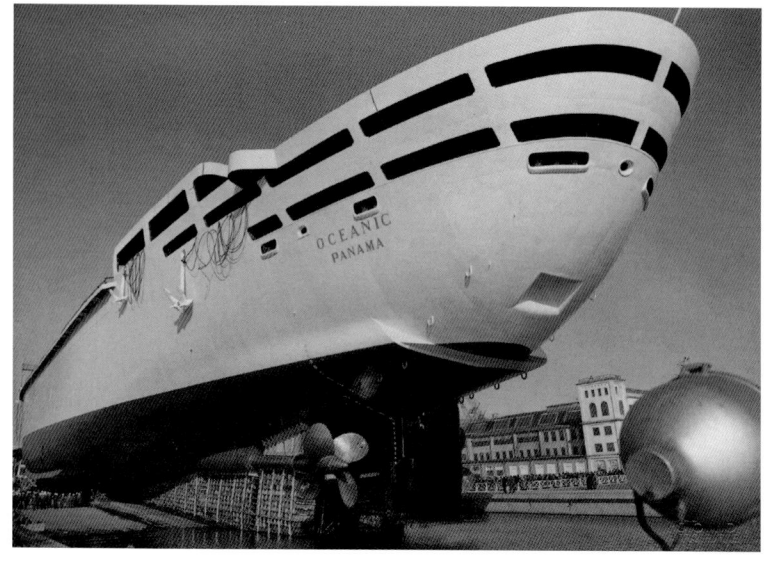

A dramatic view showing Costanzi's recently patented stern arrangement for *Oceanic*. Working with the carefully crafted bow this created a very stable, fast and fuel-efficient hull form. (Aldo Cavallini collection – naviearmatori)

Initially scheduled for 8 January 1963, *Oceanic*'s launch was postponed by one week, a delay caused by exceptionally cold winter weather. In this view the gleaming hull slides into the Adriatic having been named by Mrs Jeanna Simu, the wife of a company director. (Aldo Cavallini collection – naviearmatori)

following spring. On 28 August a press statement was released confirming the company's intentions. The news was met with a mixture of inquisitiveness and incredulity. On a practical level the new ship was already designed for quick conversion to single class cruising, so no radical modifications were required.

There has been some conjecture regarding the origins of *Oceanic*'s design, one suggestion is that it emerged from earlier plans devised for a pair of cruise ships for Aristotle Onassis, by the Dutch de Schelde yard. This is possible but seems unlikely since she was conceived as a bona fide transatlantic liner, with some off-season cruising capability. Home Lines' executive vice president, Charalambos Keusseuglou, also appears to have been influential. However ultimately it was Costanzi and his team at CRDA who took Home Line's requirements and crafted them into the maritime masterpiece that was *Oceanic*.

Although correctly lauded for its influence on future cruise ship design *Oceanic*'s layout was actually more evolutionary than revolutionary. The concept of locating the engine room

Alongside the fitting out berth in 1964. In the foreground are panels for the innovative 50 ton 'Magrodome', retractable glazed roof. (Eustachio Patalano collection – naviearmatori)

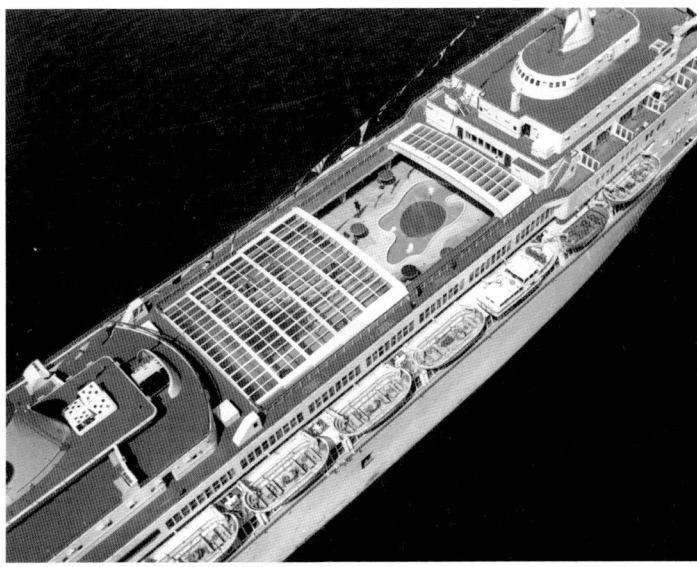

An aerial perspective with the 'Magrodome' roof half retracted demonstrating the large central area created by the three quarters aft machinery and funnel placement. The terraces of the starboard side Trianon, Alhambra and Tivoli suites can be seen in the top right. (Bill Miller collection)

53

Left: The view aft from *Oceanic*'s forward mooring deck. The superstructure was beautifully curved, raked and tiered with the frowning bridge and futuristic mast providing a powerfully purposeful summit. (itsfoto)

Below: The shapely tiered after decks descended in neat curves, superficially reminiscent of the pre-war *Normandie*. Taken from the fantail on Riviera Deck this view shows the glazed doors of the Europe Observation Lounge in the foreground. (itsfoto)

Right: *Oceanic*'s 10,350 square feet central lido area. The original concept included a single enormous pool with a narrow isthmus straddled by a small bridge. In the evening the pool would feature illuminated fountains. Presumably for practical and cost reasons these elements were subsequently dropped. Nevertheless with its twin swimming pools, striped beach mats, vibrant hued umbrellas and a little imagination it still resembled a microcosm of the Italian Riviera. (Author's collection)

Below: Passenger accommodation was spread over eight decks. The highest was Sun Deck which featured eight luxury suites with substantial terraces, named to reflect the ship's pan-European heritage, from Alhambra to Windsor. Regarded as precursors of today's proliferation of cruise ship balconies they actually echoed the terraced suites on Costanzi's first commissions, the venerable Cosulich twins *Saturnia* and *Vulcania*, which were still plying from Trieste to New York at the time. (Marc Lewis collection)

The four lower decks within the hull were almost exclusively comprised of 2, 3 and 4 berth cabin accommodation (they would have been tourist class on the Cuxhaven-Montreal service). All had private bathroom facilities and lower beds that could be converted into daytime sofas. (Marc Lewis collection)

and by association the funnel three quarters aft was not new. Shaw Savill's *Southern Cross* and P&O's *Canberra* had shown the benefits of this design in creating extensive sundeck areas amidships and public rooms below. Given the novel variations then being adopted, the funnel was perhaps the least noteworthy element of *Oceanic*'s design. Nevertheless its powerfully long, lean and low, slender ovoid shape neatly echoed the ship itself.

As with the Lloyd Triestino sisters and repeated again on *Eugenio C*, the majority of public rooms were sandwiched on a single level, between nominally First Class cabins above and Tourist class below. Named Riviera Deck, this was the hub of the ship and stretched from the Italian Hall with its views over the bow, through the adjacent Mayfair Bar, main lobby and central Aegean Room show lounge, to the Skäl Bar and elegant Europe Observation Lounge, which opened onto the fantail at the stern. Interspersed around the lobby, lounges and bars were the purser's office, two reading and writing rooms, a card room and the gift shop. The spaciousness and continuity was enhanced by locating the main central and forward stairwells on each beam, thereby creating long, central vistas. Along each flank ran an enclosed promenade, originally intended as a refuge from North Atlantic winds, the slanted glazing (presumably to assist in the smooth lowering and raising of the boats recessed above) ensured the space was showered with light, a welcome haven on blustery days in northern latitudes, as she sailed from and to New York.

The interiors were coordinated by the Venetian Giovanni 'Nino' Zoncada, who also designed several rooms, passageways and stairwells. There were cameo roles for other famed designers, including Flaminio Bini, Romano Boico, Ugo Carà, Aldo Cervi, Vittorio Frandoli, Arturo Alberto Guerello, Demetrio Hrast, Luigi Martellani, Umberto Nordio, Gio Ponti, Pierpaolo Stelo and Gustavo Pulitzer Finali. Reflecting the suite and public room names, as well as her owner's diverse backgrounds, Zoncada's overall decorative theme was pan-European, which included bas-relief depictions of the continent's many famous

Gustavo Pulitzer Finali's Italian Hall, forward on Riviera Deck, incorporated his archetypal circular forms and bold colour scheme to dramatic affect. (Marc Lewis collection)

landmarks in stairwells. Nevertheless, given the nationality of the designers, contributing artists and builder, it was inevitable that the end result was quintessential 1960s Italian. The light laminate panelling, plate glass doors, brushed aluminium balustrades, vibrant, velour clad furniture and archetypal polished linoleum flooring gave the ship a cool (in both senses of the word) feel that Americans adored.

Zoncada also commissioned the finest contemporary Italian artists including Guido Gambone, Emanuele Luzzati, Tranquillo Marangoni, Marcello Mascherini, Enrico Paulucci, Dino Predonzani, Federico Righi, and Giuseppe Zigaina. Perhaps of particular note were ceramicist Luzzati's tile encrusted walls and dome and decorative panels in the main dining room and Mascherini's figurative bronzes.

While noble and certainly ambitious the CRDA order book undeniably stretched manpower and materials to the limit. As with the Lloyd Triestino vessels a shortage of steel and surfeit of strikes prolonged the building process. Belatedly *Oceanic* embarked on her sea trials in the spring of 1965. Driven on by the 60,500 shp of her De Laval geared steam turbines the twin screws achieved a highly impressive 27.3 knots.

Having been accepted by Home Lines on 31 March 1965, *Oceanic* was stored and commenced her maiden voyage (ironically a transatlantic crossing) from Genoa on 3 April 1965. Carrying barely 200 passengers was perhaps vindication for the decision

Left: Marcello Mascherini's sculpture Nettuno e Teti (Neptune and Thetis) on the cover of a 1976 brochure. One of four bronzes the famous sculptor made for *Oceanic*, it hung in the main entrance lobby. (Marc Lewis collection)

Below: Fresh from the builders, *Oceanic* is shown moored at Trieste's Maritime Station. As was customary for CRDA built ships she was opened up for public viewing in return for donations to a nominated seaman's charity. (Author's collection)

The ship's delayed completion meant that a planned maiden cruise from Trieste to Genoa via Naples had to be cancelled. (Archivo Pietro Berti – Genova)

to abandon the transatlantic service, although it also has to be seen in the context of a one-off sailing.

The first crossing certainly proved her credentials as a fast and stable sea boat. On arrival *Oceanic* was opened to the inquisitive public and travel agents. Everyone was beguiled. Homes Lines were justifiably proud, while the wider shipping fraternity's opinion ranged from antipathy and scepticism to admiration and envy. The company had devised the sobriquet 'The ship of tomorrow', a marketing sound bite that for once had a ring of truth.

She set sail on her first seven day run to Nassau on 24 April 1965 and never looked back. Her facilities, accommodation and cuisine were rightly lauded but it was the human qualities, a warm, friendly, yet determinedly professional crew that cemented her reputation.

Right: With the customary fireboat reception, Home Lines new flagship steams past Battery Park on her maiden arrival at New York. (Marc Lewis collection)

Below: *Oceanic* arrived in the midst of a stevedore strike. With placards telling the new liner to 'Go home' (despite New York being her home port!), striking dockers reputedly threw the mooring lines back into the water several times before the ship was finally secured. (Bill Miller collection)

Marc Lewis, who sailed on her eight times in the early 1970s sums up her appeal:

> It was the crew which made the *Oceanic* and Home Lines so special. This is a major key to success that sadly today's cruise lines do not comprehend, or choose to ignore. A ship can cost US $800 million and be state-of-the-art, but it is still an amalgamation of materials; it is the crew which gives a ship its soul! To most Home Lines crew, their positions were their career and they were there for decades. They were consummate professionals who were proud of their craft. It was all Italian, including the hotel, deck and engine departments, shop personnel and all the ship's four orchestras. The moment you stepped off the gangway onto her gleaming, polished decks, for all intents and purposes, you were in Italy. And the American travelling public (especially the ladies!) loved it. Home Lines, like the similar Sitmar Cruises was a private company, they flew the Panamanian flag of convenience for tax reasons but also to keep those powerful Italian maritime unions at bay. The crew was not unionized but as compensation and inducement for this, I am certain Home Lines took very good care of them. I never heard of Home Lines ever suffering a strike or labor issue. One could easily ascertain that the *Oceanic* was a "Happy Ship"; it's just one of those intangible feelings you had when interacting with the staff. Everyone seemed very content and extremely proud of their job and reputation.

Undoubtedly that spirit emanated from the top. Captain Giovanni Ruffini was the ship's senior master for seventeen years from 1965 to 1982. Having gone to sea at fourteen on a schooner, he started with the company in 1946, earning his first command, *Argentina* just three years later as the youngest captain of a transatlantic liner. He was just thirty-five years old. An experienced and highly reputed mariner, man manager and leader, Captain Ruffini was also a consummate host, an integral part of *Oceanic*'s appeal. Keeping the passengers happy and entertained was the responsibility of cruise director Everitt E Everitt. One of the first to be appointed in such a role, EEE (as he was perhaps inevitably

The first of several trips that the Lewis family made on *Oceanic*. Marc Lewis and his parents disembark at Nassau in 1970. (Marc Lewis collection)

Captain Giovanni Ruffini (third from left) and cruise director Everitt E Everett (second from left) were significant elements of the *Oceanic* experience and played a key part in her enduring success. (Marc Lewis collection)

known), seemed to be omnipresent, attending to every fine detail to ensure guests stayed happy and entertained. The ship was also always meticulously maintained, furniture was regularly reupholstered and her white hull kept pristine.

Oceanic developed a very loyal following, a band of repeaters who created an exclusive, club-like atmosphere on many voyages. What was remarkable was Home Lines's ability to harness this loyalty on an itinerary with just a solitary port of call bracketed by five days at sea. Entertainment during those long, leisurely days was generally low-key, focusing on the Lido and its pools, supplemented by complimentary dance, Italian language lessons, or perhaps a game of cards. For the active there was a gymnasium tucked away on Sun Deck with traditional deck quoits further aft, or one could indulge in a massage or sauna. The beauty and hair dressing salons were kept busy in preparation for the soirees and two 'duty free' shops proved popular distractions, as did the latest new releases on show in the Cinema. Teenagers were catered for with their own novel 'Fun-o-rama' room and accompanying soda fountain high up on Lido deck, while younger children had their own play room and nursery on Belvedere deck. For those seeking solace or quiet contemplation there was a chapel, while of course many embarked to get away from agendas and enjoy the timeless attributes of a good book, conversation and a sea view.

Perhaps the greatest hyperbole was reserved for dining. Under the banner 'Live like a Maharajah' a 1965 brochure stated 'The kitchens and wine-cellars adjoining are a gleaming kingdom where a special corps of Europe's finest chefs prepare daily miracles of food and drink the gods of old never dreamed of in their most exalted moments!' Nevertheless food

Above: The Dining Room was reputedly the largest at sea. Devoid of pillars and with an ornate rectangular dome recess, it absorbed 650 passengers at a single sitting. (Marc Lewis collection)

Left: A beautiful menu cover depicting Christopher Columbus. The contents included Jellied essence of Pheasant, Supreme of Boston Sole Marguery and an Epicurean delicacy Steak of meadow Veal a la Diane Imperial. (Marc Lewis collection)

was inevitably a big draw and Chef Girolamo Purrone and his team provided a near endless supply for their passengers' delectation. Supplementing the two sittings of breakfast, lunch and dinner in the main restaurant was Bouillon, served on deck at 11:00 and the popular midnight buffet augmented by pizza, on offer as an appetiser at cocktails and for those with stamina at the European Lounge and Montmartre Club in the small hours. Many evenings were themed, with the Welcome and Farewell dinners bracketed by French, Italian etc nights. Repeat passengers would especially look forward to Thursday's 'Buffet Magnifique', a particularly extravagant, decorative and delicious culinary feast.

Early evening entertainment concentrated on the lounges and bars, with music and cocktails supplemented by shipboard staples such as horse racing, bingo or maybe fancy dress. Others might take in another film.

Dinner sittings were timed for 19:00 and 20:40, after which *Oceanic* really came alive. The main focus was music, provided by the ship's four resident orchestras. Despite an often elderly clientele it wasn't long before the dance floors were teeming. For those who preferred observing rather than participating a variety show of singers, dancers, conjurors and comedians performed several times a week in the Aegean Room, where the stage could be raised and lowered to improve sight lines. Having further sated themselves at the midnight buffet in the Escoffier Grill, late revellers would invariably drift aft, working off

One of *Oceanic*'s legendary buffets. It seemed possible to eat continuously all the way to Nassau and back. (Marc Lewis collection)

those extra calories to Romy Formica and the Favalosi band in the Montmartre Club. Night owls finally drifted to bed around 03:00.

In her first season *Oceanic* returned a remarkable 98 per cent load factor, perhaps even more astonishing was that in the next eighteen years she averaged 92 per cent. Profits were similarly impressive and the new flagship had repaid her construction costs by the end of the 1960s. Maiden season prices for a seven day cruise ranged from $260 to $555 per person.

At 16.00 each Saturday *Oceanic* edged away from Pier 84 and pirouetted towards the Atlantic. The precision of her weekly afternoon departures rapidly became a New York institution, as did the precursory partying. Fraught crew members trying to prepare for 1,300 new passengers would frequently be inundated with three or four times as many well-wishers. The ship became a social focal point for the Big Apple's Italian-American community.

Other than the maiden voyage she made just one more transatlantic crossing in her entire Home Lines career, returning to her builder via Palermo, Naples, Messina, Bari and Venice in June 1966, for a refit, inspection and dry-docking. Subsequent Home Lines refits were carried out at the Newport News shipyard until the late 1970s when they shifted to Bayonne New Jersey, even closer to her New York 'home'.

Although generally a smooth-running ship, *Oceanic* inevitably encountered her share of mishaps. On 3 February 1966, just ten months after entering service and shortly after arriving back at Pier 84 fire was detected. Thanks to the prompt action of sixty New York City fire-fighters the blaze was quickly contained but acrid smoke took some time to disperse from adjacent passageways. Two years later another fire almost destroyed

A vinyl record cover for the famed Zieli band, resident performers in the Italian Hall from 1967 to 1973 of such shoe tapping dance tunes as "Hully Gully Watusi".(Marc Lewis collection)

Oceanic. This time she was steaming south off the Florida coast when a ruptured oil pipe ignited, turning the engine room into an inferno. The ship's fire crew were quickly on the scene but intense heat badly damaged the machinery housing and she had to head back to New York for repairs.

By the end of the 1970s most cruise operators had decamped to Florida. The ocean liners' nemesis, jet aircraft, became the cruise ships greatest ally, flying passengers to the

Initially *Oceanic* arrived at Nassau on Tuesday morning, stayed overnight and departed on Wednesday afternoon, tying up back at Manhattan early Saturday morning. Her pendulum itinerary continued through spring, summer and autumn. (itsfoto)

Only in the depths of winter was the cycle broken with longer voyages of up to three weeks heading deep into the Caribbean. With a reduced capacity of 850 and a social columnist in tow these cruises attracted an even more sophisticated, wealthy and demanding clientele. (Marc Lewis collection)

A company Christmas card showing a rendezvous between *Oceanic* and Doric. Originally Zim Lines transatlantic flagship *Shalom, Doric* joined the Home Line fleet in 1974 and like her fleet mate earned an excellent reputation on seven night cruises, in her case to Bermuda. (Marc Lewis collection)

Throughout the 1970s *Oceanic* remained a New York stalwart, her perennial sailings a welcome constant for a city in turmoil from soaring crime, police corruption and strikes. Her success was in sharp contrast to the evaporating fleet of transatlantic liners. (itsfoto)

embarkations ports of Miami and Port Everglades. In 1982 Home Lines ordered a new cruise ship, *Atlantic*. A family resemblance was maintained in the funnel and raked mast but the new ship lacked *Oceanic's* balanced proportions. Nevertheless, she was an efficient ship and highlighted the older vessels higher operational costs.

Although initially repositioned to sail from Port Everglades on her winter Caribbean itineraries, *Oceanic* proved less successful in the new cruise order and was laid up at Newport News over the winter of 1982/3. When Home Lines invited tenders for another new vessel (*Homeric*), the eighteen-year-old *Oceanic*, the ship that had redefined modern cruising, was put on the sale's list. Chandris, Sun Line and Norwegian Caribbean Lines all looked at her but it was to be two years later, in August 1985 that she was eventually purchased by relative newcomers, Premier Cruise Line. On 21 November, having returned from her final Home Lines Cruise, Oceanic sailed to Newport News and a $10 million refurbishment.

Premier had entered into a mutually beneficial arrangement with the Disney Corporation, in which four- or seven-day Caribbean itineraries could be linked with stays at the Florida theme parks. There was a brief charter as an exposition ship at Boston in 1987 but otherwise 'Starship' *Oceanic* settled into a year-round cycle of short cruises. Her pseudonym of the 'Mickey Mouse Ship' became an affectionate rather than a derogatory sobriquet.

In 1990 *Oceanic* was re-registered at Nassau (previously it had been Panama). The ship's success prompted Disney to start planning its own cruise operation which would come to fruition by the turn of the century, so switching studios Premier formed an alliance with Warner Brothers in 1993. Four years later the company was acquired by Cruise Holdings, merging with that corporation's existing Dolphin and Seawind brands to create Premier Cruises. She adopted a new, deeper red hull and began being marketed as 'Big Red Boat'.

After five months of cosmetic surgery, on 25 April 1986 the briefly renamed *Royale Oceanic* sailed from Port Canaveral on her first four day itinerary. Although structurally unchanged, the vivid red hull livery was indicative of a very different clientele. (Lucinda McGrew collection)

Sticking with the Disney theme, 'Pluto's playhouse' was created by amalgamating the former children's room and nursery with the underutilised Garden Lounge on Belvedere (now Premier) Deck. A circular children's pool was built on the adjacent terrace. (Lucinda McGrew collection)

Gleaming chrome and pastel shades abounded in the remodelled public rooms. This is the Tropicana Club adjacent to the Lido, formerly the Portofino Bar. (Lucinda McGrew collection)

Despite taking liberties with their ships' names the new operation was generally welcomed by ship enthusiasts for keeping a fleet of aging liners sailing in their dotage.

Alas what the gleaming new behemoths of the competition might have lacked in aesthetics they made up for in efficiency, facilities, and accommodation. Premier Cruises became increasingly uncompetitive and in the spring of 2000 *Oceanic* was sent to Freeport, Grand Bahama for another refit. An internet café, together with new child and teenager facilities were added and all public rooms refurbished, however Premier was already financially ailing and in September the company suspended operations. The thirty-five-year-old *Oceanic* was seized on behalf of creditors before sailing to lay-up at Freeport, where she joined *Big Red*

Boat II (originally Costa's *Eugenio C*) and the rest of the Premier ships. Silent and still this moribund fleet awaited the inevitable final voyage to the scrap yards of the East.

Oceanic's reprieve came from a most unlikely source. Around the turn of the millennium several tour operators (notably Saga, Thompson and Airtours) which had previously acted in a purely agency capacity created their own cruise lines. The largest Spanish operator, Pullmantur decided to follow and in early 2001 were looking for a suitable vessel. *Oceanic*

In October 1994 'Star Ship' *Oceanic* made her first transatlantic crossing in almost three decades, to Genoa for a major two month refit. In addition to engine room and air conditioning upgrades, the new 'Tiki' bar was added at the stern and public rooms and accommodation were refurbished. (photo by the late Carlo Martinelli reproduced with kind permission of 'Captain Haddock'- naviearmatori)

Oceanic was chosen to inaugurate Pullmantur's cruise ship operations. Purchased in May 2001, she was refitted at Cadiz, then sailed from Barcelona to Villefranche (seen here), Livorno, Civitavecchia, Palermo and Tunis. Later the Sicilian call was replaced by Valetta, which was in turn superseded by Naples. (Paco Diaz Guerrero collection)

fitted the bill perfectly. There was an element of 'back to the future', as she embarked on a year-round programme of seven-night cruises.

Oceanic became a favourite among Spanish-speaking cruise goers, a fun-filled, vibrant success. Over ensuing years she attracted a broad range of passengers from across the age and social spectrum. Pullmantur expanded, rapidly, acquiring an eclectic mix of second-hand tonnage while constantly upgrading *Oceanic* to comply with the impending 2010 SOLAS regulations.

Pullmantur's meteoric rise made it a very attractive proposition and so in September 2006 the company was acquired by RCI. The forty year old *Oceanic* initially remained an important element of the Pullmantur fleet, however RCI, like Carnival, soon shifted older tonnage from its own fleet into the emerging business. In 2009 *Oceanic* was earmarked for a revised programme of shorter cruises prior to disposal at the end of the summer season. However as Spain teetered on the edge of solvency the company was inevitably affected by the Eurozone crisis in 2008/9. In early March the programme was cancelled. *Oceanic* it transpired had been sold to a Panamanian concern and departed Barcelona on 19 March 2009 under charter to the Japanese Peaceboat organisation. It seemed a fitting role for a vessel which had inspired so much affection over four decades.

On 26 June 2009, as part of her first voyage, *Oceanic* made a much publicised return to the finger piers of New York. Regrettably, the prodigal's homecoming was tainted by news that US coastguard inspectors had identified a total of seventeen safety violations. These included a crack in the hull, probably resulting from an incident during her Icelandic call. Initially divers patched her up before *Oceanic* was taken to the Bayonne New Jersey shipyard for dry-docking and permanent repairs. She left on 2 July 2009, sailing south to Panama then up to Vancouver where an oil spillage caused more bad publicity. With a sense of relief she finally returned to Yokohoma.

The Peaceboat programme continued unabated over the next three years, visiting new ports in a broad spectrum of countries (although notably avoiding North America). As a

Oceanic sailed from Yokohama on her first circumnavigation, taking a westerly course via Suez and Northern Europe. There was a maiden call at Le Havre, ironically one of the terminal ports for Home Lines aborted transatlantic service. The Norwegian fjords and Iceland provided stunning scenic backdrops to the organisations laudable work of fostering tolerance, harmony and practical understanding across the globe. (Author's collection)

disciple of peace there was a certain irony in press reports of a pirate attack off the Yemini coastline in 2010. Brandishing AK-47s, the attackers approached the vulnerable cruise ship in speedboats while Captain Teodor Candrlic and his crew put well-rehearsed drills into practice. In the engine room engineers responded to the Captain's demand and *Oceanic*'s ageing turbines ratcheted up until she was apparently steaming at about 25 knots, lurching on a zig-zag course. Meanwhile brave deckhands trained high pressure hoses to repel the assailants. Continuing at top speed Oceanic out-ran the modern day buccaneers and ultimately found protection from a patrolling NATO warship. After almost fifty years of relative containment her powerful engines proved their worth.

In early 2012 Peaceboat announced the acquisition of *Ocean Dream,* originally Carnival's *Tropicale,* while rumours circulated that *Oceanic* may be retained for voyages in the Asian area.

In fact after returning to Japan in early May she was de-stored and briefly laid-up. As the final incarnation of 1960s Italian shipbuilding genius and particularly since her classic profile was unaltered by subsequent 'enhancements' she would have made a wonderful candidate for preservation. Undoubtedly the global financial crises put paid to any such thoughts. Forsaking the beaches of Alang *Oceanic* was sold to scrappers at Zhoushan in China, where within months she had disappeared, leaving fond memories of one of the most beautiful and popular passenger ships of all time.

On 24 January 2012 *Oceanic* cast off from Yokohoma on what would be her final Peaceboat circumnavigation. Her normally spotless paintwork was starting to look a little tardy and reports indicated her interiors were similarly careworn. (Author's collection)

4

Eugenio C

If Costanzi and Zoncada had already established themselves among the pantheon of great exterior and interior ship designers with *Oceanic*, their final collaborative project would cement that legacy.

Costa Line, whose eponymous founders had emerged in the post-war era as leading migrant carriers to Central and South America, were looking for a new flagship. Nominally she was a replacement for *Bianca C*, the 18,427 grt former Messagerie Maritimes and Arosa Line vessel that had capsized off Grenada in October 1961 following an engine room fire. The insurance pay-out for the loss proved instrumental in funding her successor, which they entrusted to CRDA rather than the Ansaldo yard at Sestri Ponente near Genoa, which had produced her predecessor *Federico C*.

Although *Eugenio C* is often referred to as *Oceanic*'s near sister there were quite significant external and internal differences between the two. Quite apart from the hull's shape and sheer, Costanzi and Zoncada's jointly conceived, beautifully raked and

(Author's collection – www.sarniawatercolours.co.uk)

In order to qualify for shipbuilding subsidies the first keel plate of yard number 1884 was ceremoniously laid on 4 January 1964, just four months after the building contract had been signed. Given the inherent time pressures CRDA utilised a version of *Galileo Galilei*'s hull (updated to include the hybrid stern), blended with *Oceanic*'s power plant and general layout. (Aldo Cavallini collection – naviearmatori)

The 217.39 metre (712 foot) hull was named by Donna Pinuccia, wife of company President Angelo Costa on 21st November 1964. Dressed overall with signal flags from stern to stern, like many Italian launchings she was painted in red oxide primer. Some forty years later she would again don a red hull. (Aldo Cavallini collection – naviearmatori)

rounded forward superstructure differed considerably from her predecessor. Comprising a single, curved four-deck-high block with integrated, swept back bridge wings, the sculpted bulkhead seamlessly wrapped around into the glazed promenade. This was quite unlike *Oceanic*'s tiered arrangement with its separate 'island' housing the bridge, officer's accommodation, and luxury suites. Even at the stern the aft decks more closely resembled *Galileo Galilei*'s squared arrangement than *Oceanic*'s series of concentric curves.

Then of course there were those funnels. Original design drawings show a single *Oceanic*-type stack and another proposal considered a narrow cone-like structure incorporating a pronounced scoop. Ultimately, drawing obvious comparisons with the earlier *Rotterdam* and *Canberra*, *Eugenio C* had twin stacks, positioned 'tanker style' athwart the ship. Designed by the same Turin Polytechnic team under the stewardship of

Professor Carlo Mortarini that was responsible for *Michelangelo* and *Raffaello* and the Lloyd Triestino twins, each funnel was topped by a small grille and soot shield arrangement, to optimise airflow and smoke dispersal. As with the fins on the French Line's mighty *France*, ingenious use of dampers meant that in the event of a cross wind exhaust smoke could be channelled solely through the downwind pipe.

Left: A study of perfect symmetry and one of the most evocative (and intimidating) advertising photographs ever. In its simple, streamlined form, *Eugenio C*'s forward bulkhead and swept back bridge wings were reminiscent of some of the great pre-war liners, such as *Normandie*, *Conte di Savoia*, *Bremen* and *Europa*. (Author's collection)

Below: Installing *Eugenio C*'s distinctive 'tanker style' stacks. The basic slender pipe arrangement was given a dash of Italian chic by being raked, tapered and incorporating a pronounced outward slant. (Aldo Cavallini collection – naviearmatori)

Right: *Eugenio C*'s thick-set radar mast neatly complemented the funnels, echoing their basic sculptured shape and rake. (Author's collection)

Below: *Eugenio C*'s CRDA-De Laval geared turbines under construction at the Fabbrica Macchine Sant'Andrea's workshop in Trieste. (Aldo Cavallini collection – naviearmatori)

Much of *Eugenio C*'s enduring fame was linked to her exceptional speed. Under the watchful guidance of Chief Engineer Angelo Roncallo she achieved a creditable 28.43 knots in the course of trials. Cesare Zaniboni, who rose through the ranks on *Eugenio C* and eventually became direttore di macchina and construction supervisor at Fincantieri, provides a wonderful insight into the processes involved and sensations experienced in what to many remains the most mysterious and alien realm of all, the engine room:

> During manoeuvres, in addition to the normal watch (two Officers, two Firemen, two Greasers, one Electrician and one *Frigorista*) there was generally the *direttore di macchina*, the Chief Engineer and the First Electrician. The crew responded to telegraph messages from the Bridge by turning the wheels, which opened the valves that brought steam to the turbines, the larger one was for ahead movement, while the smaller one was for astern. A mechanical system prevented the two valves from opening at the same time. The officer in charge monitored the activity of the three boilers through the gauges and dials on the instrument panel and indicated at what speed the operators could turn the wheel in order to respond to the orders from the Bridge, while not overloading the steam generators. All this had to be carried out with impressive coordination, the result of constant teaching and repetition. Viewed from the outside, the scene was reminiscent of a conductor and an orchestra: given the high noise of the room, everything was coordinated with hand gestures, as though the turbine operators were following a score.

Quoted in *Meditelegraph* in June 2015 Signor Zaniboni's evokes a tender portrait of the deep bond between the crew and their ship:

> It had a unique character, the *Eugenio*; you needed to be intimately acquainted with her, if you wanted to be able to handle her. To be an officer on board meant to be at the forefront of Italian naval expertise. It was an endless learning experience.

Eugenio C's engine room in the course of maneuvers. The operator in the foreground turns the wheel, introducing steam to the turbine under the supervision of the centrally placed officer. Cesare Zaniboni eloquently describes the experience; 'the sensations were similar to those you have driving a high-level sports car ... in short it was like driving a Ferrari and the adrenaline levels experienced are, I think, in the memory of all those who were lucky enough to work on a ship like the *Eugenio C*.' (Cesare Zaniboni collection)

It was with immense pride that *Eugenio C* was formally accepted by Linea C on 22 August 1966, and welcomed into Genoa. The next day she departed on a shakedown cruise to Cannes, Barcelona and Lisbon, before returning to her home port for provisioning. On 31 August 1966, with Captain Marco Simicich in command, *Eugenio C* was accorded a spectacular send off on her maiden voyage to South America. After calling at Cannes and Barcelona she made her final European landfall at Lisbon on 3 September. To the backdrop of the glittering lights of the Portuguese capital she departed at midnight, glided under the brand new Salazar Bridge, and out into the Atlantic.

The following morning those fortunate first passengers woke to sample the delights of life at sea on board the Costa flagship. A relatively smooth crossing was guaranteed thanks to the installation of two pairs of Denny-Brown fin stabilisers, as she gathered pace on a south-westerly course for Brazil. Accommodation was provided for a total of 1,659 passengers. Reflecting the requirements of what remained a significant emigrant trade, only 214 berths were for First Class passengers, located on Sun and Boat decks.

All First Class cabins had private facilities. The residual 1,445 berths were sub-divided into the equivalent of second and third class, although in the more egalitarian times these were actually called Tourist A and Tourist B. Located in a quieter, central position the 374 Tourist A passengers occupied larger cabins, with their own en suite facilities. The residual 1,071 Tourist B passengers were housed in four to eight berth cabins, primarily in the fore and aft parts of the hull. Many of these had their own bathrooms but 122 cabins used communal baths and toilets.

Eugenio C at Genoa early in her career. Her home port was just a short distance from the ancestral homeland of Santa Margherita Ligure, where the Costa family's olive oil business had started and thrived. (itsfoto)

The first class accommodation included eight luxury apartments named after famous Italian resorts. Situated at the front of the superstructure, the four largest suites featured a living room, curtained off bedroom and large bathroom and also had full height picture windows, offering panoramic views over the bow. (Marc Lewis collection)

Although class divisions were nominally reminiscent of days gone by, Tourist B was far from steerage and to impoverished emigrants offered a level of accommodation and facilities exceeding any previous experience. (Marc Lewis collection)

With the exception of restaurants, the main public rooms for all passengers were located on Salon deck. Perhaps inevitably Costa entrusted the interior design and décor almost exclusively to Nino Zoncada, who had so successfully fulfilled the role on *Federico C. Eugenio C* was arguably the pinnacle of his career, with a series of eight, elegant, modern and beautifully furnished public rooms. Harmonious and coherent were the adjectives most often associated with the new flagship's décor, avoiding the sometimes jarring contrasts that resulted when a disparate team of

In common with most Italian Liners of the era there was extensive outdoor deck space and swimming pools provided for each of the three classes. (Author's collection)

The first class lido area was located amidships. Given her tropical itinerary it was decided not to incorporate a Magrodome sliding roof arrangement seen on *Oceanic*, however all the outdoor areas benefited from considerable glass screening as protection from buffeting Atlantic winds. (Author's collection)

designers were employed. All the rooms were named and themed around precious or semi-precious stones, progressing aft from the First Class Ambra Ballroom, through the Rubino and Opale lounge amidships to the expansive Turchese Lounge and Ballroom. Combining colour coordinated velour chairs and curtains, Zoncada also championed the best contemporary Italian artists, commissioning works by Massimo Campigti in the Ambra Lounge, Emmanuele Luzzati in the Rubino Lounge and Marcello Maschierini in the Turchese and Opale Lounges. There was much less distinction between the public rooms of the three classes than was evident on contemporary Italian Line tonnage, consequently she was easily convertible to one class cruising. The ship had a warm and luxuriant atmosphere.

The oval shaped Ambra Lounge was arguably Zoncada's signature room, occupying the forward part of Promenade Deck. Formed by the ship's forward bulkhead with large picture windows on three sides, this was the one lounge with direct sea views. All the other lounges were surrounded by a traditional enclosed promenade, part of which was set aside as a lush winter garden. (Marc Lewis collection)

Despite many Costa brochures lacking human occupants (giving the appearance of a modern day *Marie Celeste*!), there were plenty of interesting distractions for passengers of all classes and ages on the voyage south. The cinema/theatre showed the very latest international film releases. (Author's collection)

Teenagers had their own room with a bowling alley and pinball machines. (Author's collection)

Their parents might be sunbathing on the Lido (*bottom*) or wrapped up with a good book along the enclosed promenade. The Tourist 'A' Lido area and swimming pool occupied the aft section of *Ponte Sol* (Sun Deck). (Author's collection)

Meal times were always a high point of the day. The three restaurants were decoratively similar forming a horseshoe around the kitchen. This picture shows diners in the 'Magic flute' First Class dining room. (Author's collection)

Looking after the passengers was a crew of 424. Like their Italian Line and Lloyd Triestino counterparts they broadly reflected the nation's regional divisions, with the majority of stewards and hotel staff drawn from Naples and Campania, while many officers hailed from Genoa and Liguria.

As on all liners at that time crew recreation was limited, both in terms of time and opportunity. However with tours of duty lasting up to eighteen months, bonds between crew members were forged that have endured for a lifetime. 'There was little time to kill. At most one took a stroll to have a smoke or a breath of fresh air. The crew would congregate at the bar in the evenings, perhaps listening to soccer games on the short wave radio. While horsing around was common, brawls were infrequent. Each lived the life at sea in their own way'.

Following her spectacular fireboat reception at Rio de Janeiro, *Eugenio C* skirted the Brazilian coast to Santos, before heading south to the River Plate and its sentinel capital cities Montevideo and Buenos Aires. She stayed three days in the Argentine capital, with a reputed 15,000 people making the traditional donation to seaman's charities in return for a glimpse inside.

Somewhat ironically, given Constanzi's role in resolving similar problems on Italia's *Michelangelo* and *Raffaello*, Costa's one initial concern about their new flagship was vibration. Cavitation was the culprit and so new six-bladed propellers were fitted during her first dry-docking in October 1967, which resolved the issue. The advent of *Eugenio C* resulted in a reshuffle of tonnage throughout the Costa fleet. Although a theoretical replacement for *Bianca C*, *Eugenio C* had taken over the South America service from former flagship *Federico C*, which repositioned to *Bianca C's* Central and North America service. *Eugenio C's* running mate in her new role was the recently acquired 15,889 ton former SGTM (Societé Générale de Transports Maritime) liner *Provence*. Acquired as *Enrico C* in 1965 Costa sent her to the Marriotti yard for a $12 million rebuild and she made her maiden voyage to South America just three months before *Eugenio C*, on 23 May 1966. Although

Right: A personal favourite and amongst the finest publicity photographs ever. *Eugenio C* steams towards the South Atlantic at over 27 knots. (Marc Lewis collection)

Below: Shortly after 7 a.m. on 9th September *Eugenio C* entered the port of Rio de Janeiro, rounded Sugar Loaf Mountain and docked in the shadows of Corcovado, under the gaze of the iconic statue of Christ the Redeemer. Her passage time from Lisbon had been six and a half days, averaging 27.45 knots. This was the last of the trans-ocean speed records to be broken by a liner on regular service and unlike the Blue Riband of the North Atlantic has never been bettered by another passenger vessel. (Author's collection)

only half the size and unable to match her pace, *Enrico C* proved to be a dependable and popular consort in the face of direct competition from the Italian Line's *Augustus* and *Giulio Cesare*.

Eugenio C also proved herself to be a fine cruise ship. Her first such voyage was a 34 night, fifteen port circumnavigation of continental Africa, which left Genoa on 9 January 1967. Repeated the following year, the liner was soon seen in a range of locations as diverse itineraries incorporated calls at Mediterranean, Caribbean, African, North European and even Pacific ports. By the mid-1970s she was spending increased time on the single class cruise circuit but nevertheless included half a dozen round trip voyages to Buenos Aires per year.

The Costa flagship quickly settled into her new role and was the most popular vessel on the La Plata run. First class was the preserve of the well-heeled and well connected including captains of business, diplomats and senior church officials as well as wealthy travellers. Tourist A and B primarily attracted their subordinates, emigrants (southbound), reverse migrants (northbound) and tourists. (Author's collection)

Eugenio C digs her nose into an Atlantic swell, Northbound from Rio to Lisbon (Vladimiro Fiorchi collection)

Eugenio C at Oslo, berthed under the ramparts of Akershus Castle. As a former crew member recalls 'A Costa cruise in those days was relatively expensive and exclusive, the passengers on board *Eugenio C* were rich people.' (itsfoto)

On 3 October 1977 *Eugenio C* cast off from Genoa with 850 passengers on a very special voyage, her maiden world circumnavigation. Heading east, she made for Alexandria before transiting the Suez Canal on route to Bombay and Colombo on the Indian sub-continent. In South East Asia she called at Penang, Singapore, Bangkok, Manila and Hong Kong. Skirting the Chinese coast she set course for Kobe and Yokohama before crossing the Pacific, to Honolulu. Sweeping under the Golden Gate Bridge, *Eugenio C* made landfall on the American continent at San Francisco, then Los Angeles, the Mexican ports of Acapulco and Cartagena and after passing through the Panama Canal stopped at St Thomas, before steaming directly to Genoa.

Also in 1977 the state-funded shipping conglomerate FINMARE's retrenchment program was in full swing. This included the withdrawal of Italian Line services to La Plata, then entrusted to the popular *Cristoforo Colombo* and making the very last liner voyage, *Guglielmo Marconi*. With *Enrico C* ostensibly a full-time cruise ship, *Eugenio C* maintained the maritime link between Europe and South America alone, Costa briefly benefiting from an influx of the shrinking shipboard clientele. Nevertheless aircraft competition was now firmly established, eroding all semblance of the halcyon days.

In 1982, three crossings took place, but Costa was forced to cancel a fourth due to the Falkland's War. This was particularly pertinent given her resemblance to *Canberra*, the British troop ship affectionately known as the Great White Whale, which was then steaming in the South Atlantic filled with Paratroopers and Marines.

From 1983, all demarcation barriers between the classes were permanently removed as *Eugenio C* became a full-time cruise ship. Nevertheless for die-hards and romanticists two repositioning 'liner' voyages were on offer per year, southbound in the autumn and northbound in the spring between Genoa and Buenos Aires. During her long career *Eugenio C*'s endured her share of mishaps and scares. Quite apart from storms, like the one endured at the end of the 1978 world cruise, there was a grounding in the Mississippi and an engine room fire. However arguably the most infamous incident

Above: Eugenio C departing Genoa. By the end of the 1970s she was the only three class liner left in service and one of the very few making regular, scheduled, transoceanic crossings. The maritime link between Europe and South America was dying, an inevitable consequence of the acceleration of modern living. (Pascal Jammes collection)

Left: After the success of the first circumnavigation *Eugenio C* embarked on another in 1978, which included a rare and much anticipated call at Shanghai, in the then reclusive People's Republic of China. The cruise was also noteworthy for the storm encountered as she approached the English Channel en route to Southampton. Although structurally undamaged, the tempest left a trail of destruction, including upturned pianos and thirty broken limbs. (Pascal Jammes collection)

occurred on Boxing Day 1984. At 9 pm that evening, having recently left Rio de Janeiro on a post-Christmas cruise, the Costa flagship was heading dead slow out of port when passengers noted the ship judder. It transpired two Brazilian warships on manoeuvres in the area had strayed into the exit channel reserved for merchant shipping. One, the veteran destroyer *Sergipe*, struck the *Eugenio C*'s bow and scraped along to a point just below the bridge wing before the two vessels became disentangled. To assess for damage, the Costa flagship turned about and returned to Rio where repairs were affected while passengers remained on board.

As *Eugenio C* sailed into her third decade of service Costa planned a series of modifications designed to secure her new role in the highly competitive global cruise market. In October 1986, she was taken to the Marriotti shipyard where her powerful turbines were de-rated to a maximum output of 39,000 shp. Despite this she was subsequently no slouch, still capable of 24 knots. Further mechanical changes included the installation of a bow thruster to assist manoeuvring in the tight confines of cruise ports and anchorages. The galleys were gutted and the most modern food preparation and distribution equipment installed, while 70 of the original 122 'no facility' cabins were provided with bathrooms. Externally the most visible alteration was at the stern, where the now redundant Tourist B swimming pool and lido was replaced by a full-sized tennis court (one of very few aboard a ship, most famously on the top decks of the pre-war *Normandie* and *Empress of Britain*). On 1 December 1987, bearing the name *Eugenio Costa* and sporting new blue and yellow hull sheer stripes to assimilate her into the rebranded Costa fleet, the refurbished liner re-entered service.

Within a year the new tennis court would be consumed and raised one deck by the largest single element of refurbishment expenditure. At the Marriotti yard in October 1987, the prefabricated structure was hoisted aboard and welded into place. (Photo by Enrico Polidori – Captain Haddock collection – naviearmatori)

Over the next seven years she toured the globe, her elegant lines in sharp contrast to the bulky profiles of her more modern fleet mates. Nevertheless looks do not bring profits and her aging, thirsty turbines and high crew ratio meant she was an expensive ship to run.

The aborted American Family Cruises refit of October 1994 was used instead to implement a $20 million refurbishment at the INMA yard at La Spezia. On completion of the work, at the beginning of December, she left Genoa for Buenos Aires and the start of a winter cruise program. In fact as she steamed for the South Atlantic it transpired *Eugenio Costa* was under new ownership and flying the Liberian flag. Costa Crociere was in a state of transition. Under the stewardship of company chairman and patriarch Nicola Costa (among other attributes he was a concert cellist with the Genoa Philarmonic Orchestra) the line had borrowed heavily to compete head on with the industry's major players. To help fund that new investment *Eugenio Costa* was now the property of Mascot Shipping SA of

Above left: Although neatly curved and painted to blend in with the stepped after decks, the new 600 seat show lounge inevitably slightly marred the ship's original profile. The adjoining former Tourist B public rooms, including the original Turchese Lounge, were transformed into an open plan 'Piazza'. (Aldo Cavallini collection)

Above right: In 1993 Costa earmarked *Eugenio Costa* to be refitted as *American Pioneer* for its short-lived joint venture with American Family Cruises. Under the plans the former Ambra lounge on newly named Entertainment Deck would have been divided in two, the 'Rock-o-saurus Club' for 5 to 7 year olds to port and 'Fuzzy-wuzzy's Den' for 2 to 4 year olds to starboard. The operation closed down in September 1994, just weeks before the refit was due to start. (Marc Lewis collection)

Monrovia, a subsidiary of the Bremer Vulkan shipyard. She had been sold in part payment of a new 76,000-ton sister to the recently completed *Costa Victoria*.

Under the terms of the sale, Costa chartered their former flagship back, to complete her scheduled programme through until the end of October 1996. With former running mate *Enrico Costa* also sold, *Eugenio Costa* was the last classic liner in a very different looking fleet.

Unceremoniously, *Eugenio Costa* was laid up at Genoa on 1 November 1996, having completed her final Mediterranean cruise. That same autumn *Canberra* was retired and sent to the scrap yards of Gaddani Beach, Pakistan, indirectly giving her Italian counterpart a reprieve. On 12 February 1997 *Eugenio Costa* was purchased by UK-based Lowline Shipping, Bremer Vulkan having gone into insolvency the previous year. Regrettably it was a scenario repeated several times during the rest of her career, as though the ship was cursed as a portent of financial ruin.

Her first employment, between January and March 1998, was on one night gambling cruises out of New York. With assorted shipyard detritus littering the former First Class lido it was hardly the most salubrious start to her new career.

Nevertheless Lowline had secured a long term charter to a new player in the UK cruise market, Direct Cruises. As a spin-off from the highly successful Direct Holidays the concept was simple, by marketing cruises straight to the public the company avoided paying agent's commission and could pass those savings on to the customer, thereby undercutting competitors. They cited the withdrawal of *Canberra* and CTC's *Southern Cross* as creating a void in the market, their aim was to offer a service comparable to P&O's *Victoria*, at CTC prices. A further selling point was the decision to position *Edinburgh Castle* out of Liverpool and Greenock (close to the company headquarters in Glasgow), harnessing a perceived untapped market in the north of England and Scotland. Within weeks the programme was sold out, so *Apollon*, originally Canadian Pacific's *Empress of Canada* was drafted in.

Having completed her New York programme *Edinburgh Castle* steamed across the Atlantic, arriving at Cammell Laird's Birkenhead yard on 31 March 1998 for finishing touches. Regrettably the initial optimism was short-lived. Thirty passengers (from a complement of

Even in her dotage *Eugenio C* was gaining new admirers. Ugo Nuzzo joined the crew in 1996 'I was the ship's photographer and worked for about nine months until they sold the ship. A lot of crew were from Peru, Chile and Honduras .... they had parties in the crew bar with South American music. Often it was the priest on board who organised the parties.' (Ugo Nuzzo collection)

Lowline Shipping's new acquisition was sent for a further refit, emerging as *Edinburgh Castle* with an all-white livery and an attractive deep blue and yellow funnel. (Author's collection)

over a thousand) understandably refused to travel on *Edinburgh Castle*'s maiden voyage from Liverpool after a burst pipe flooded several cabins. Of course those 3 per cent garlanded the headlines, while by all accounts the majority of the remaining 97 per cent had a largely enjoyable holiday. Teething problems are an inevitable part of any new shipping venture but the unwanted and often unwarranted criticism from a merciless press proved disproportionately harmful. Mechanical and plumbing problems plagued that maiden season, disrupting schedules and involving costly repairs while *Apollon* was similarly afflicted, her early cruises cancelled through a combination of boiler breakdowns and delays in fitting out.

Just as she appeared to be settling into her new role, *Edinburgh Castle* suffered a complete loss of electrical power on 24 May 1998, when her main switchboard short-circuited. Although temporarily rectified, it was decided to return to Liverpool and the ship was sent for permanent repairs. With full refunds, compensation and the offer of a free ten day cruise, passengers could hardly complain, yet inevitably some still did.

Further electrical problems in September compounded the problem, so that on 14 October, at the end of her advertised cruise programme, the ship arrived at Southampton for repairs and an extensive two month overhaul. For Lowline Shipping it was the final straw, the costly refit also deprived the company of a lucrative charter. After being placed under arrest for unpaid debts Lowline went into receivership. Ownership of *Edinburgh Castle* passed to their biggest creditor, Cammell Laird.

On completion of a further reputed US$25 million overhaul, Cammell Laird chartered their new acquisition to Premier Cruise Lines in 1999. At least she found herself in familiar company, Premier had become the ultimate destination for an assortment of 1950s and 1960s vintage liners, including fellow Italian's *Oceanic* and *Federico C* but also *Rotterdam*, *Transvaal Castle* and *Infante dom Henrique*. Sporting a bright red hull and renamed *The Big Red Boat II*, the erstwhile *Eugenio C* sailed from New York on a seven night summer season of cruises to Newport, Boston, Halifax and St Johns. If her body remained broadly intact it appeared her soul had been sold. Once again however she had gravitated towards a company on the brink of insolvency.

In June 1998 it transpired that two former passengers had contracted Legionnaires disease. Whilst no direct link could be traced to the ship, sample testing identified traces of legionella bacteria in the drinking water storage. When the ship docked at Greenock on 28 June 1998 the system was purified but with the BBC headlining 'UK passengers leave legionnaire liner'. Edinburgh Castle's reputation was in tatters. (Prolla collection – naviearmatori)

Cammell Laird retained ownership of the ship and actively sought further charters, while keeping her well maintained. Among prospective buyers were representatives of the newly formed Pullmantur Cruises but the Spaniards were ultimately put off by her costly, temperamental machinery, deciding to purchase the slightly older but more reliable *Oceanic* instead. In 2003, Cammell Laird finally sold the *Big Red Boat II* to Argo Ship Management

In September 2000 Premier Cruises went into liquidation, *Big Red Boat II* was briefly chartered to the US Government before joining her redundant fleet mates in lay-up at Freeport. (Roberto Mazzoli collection – naviearmatori)

but the new owners were also unable to secure a charter. Maintenance was compromised and the ship's condition rapidly deteriorated. That final voyage to the breakers became inevitable. With the abbreviated name *Big Red*, her departure from Freeport in April 2005 was notable for the great plumes of dense black smoke which drifted across the port from her twin funnels.

Under her own steam, she crossed the Atlantic, bunkered in the Azores and continued east, to India, anchoring off Alang on 5 June 2005. Two days later, she weighed anchor and was beached. As her keel shuddered to a standstill 'finished with engines' was rung up for a final time.

A carcass on the debris-strewn sands, the former *Eugenio C* succumbs to the breakers. (Aldo Cavallini collection – naviearmatori)

How we all prefer to remember her. *Eugenio C* heads out into the Atlantic on another ocean crossing. (Pascal Jammes collection)

Epilogue

The four ships featured here are now long gone, however they retain a loyal following to this day, with social media bringing together former crew members, passengers and interested interlopers like myself. We reminisce and wallow in dewy-eyed nostalgia, remembering experiences enjoyed, endured or (in my case) imagined. Tangible memory joggers are preserved thanks to a plethora of ephemera, memorabilia and the perseverance of a select band of intrepid collectors who retrieve elements of the ships themselves, including artwork and furniture from the scrap yards of Asia.

As for Costanzi, more than half a century has passed since his death but he is far from forgotten. There is a rather undistinguished street in Monfalcone named after him but more appropriate and enduring memorials include exhibits at the local Museo Della Cantieristica Monfalcone and online at Italianliners.com. Thanks to Stephen Payne, *Queen Mary 2*'s stern brought Costanzi's name back to prominence and introduced him to a new generation of shipping enthusiasts. Nevertheless perhaps his greatest legacy has been the perpetuation and growth of the Monfalcone shipyard into one of the world's foremost cruise ship building facilities. It would, one senses, give him satisfaction to know the yard he worked so hard to save remains at the very cutting edge of passenger ship design and construction.

Acknowledgements

I am once again indebted to the generosity of a broad spectrum of friends and acquaintants, old and new, enduring and fleeting, who have helped to make this book possible. Many thanks to Connor Stait and all at Amberley for accepting the project and helping to make it a reality, especially in these challenging times. A special mention for Marc Lewis whose numerous insights and countless images have been invaluable, especially regarding *Oceanic*. Others who kindly helped with pictures, anecdotes and/or other material include Scott Babus, Pietro Berti, G Boato, Nicolo Campus, Piero Casiglia, Aldo Cavallini Josephine Cicio, Paul M Creutz, Mike Dale, Renato Michelina Dore, Dante Flore, Vladimiro Fiorchi, Maurizio Gadda, Carmello Francesco Grasso, Paco Diaz Guerrero, 'Captain Haddock', Don Hazeldine, Alberto Imparato, Italianliners.com, Pascal Jammes, Uwe Jespersen, Dennis Kenna, Roberto Mazzoli, Lucinda McGrew, Bill Miller, Mario Minuto, Francesco Mistretta, Museo dela cantieristica Monfalcone, Ugo Nuzzo, Dr Stephen Payne MBE, Eustachio Patalano via naviearmatori, Dr Bruce Peter, Prolla, Alfredo Salomini, Claudio Savino, Claudio Serra, Silvia Tomarchio and Cesare Zaniboni. Every attempt has been made to seek permission for copyright material included in this book. However, if we have inadvertently used copyright material without permission or acknowledgement the author and publisher apologise and will make the necessary correction at the first opportunity.

I would like to thank friends and family (especially Janice, Alex, Becca and Mum) for their ongoing support and also those readers whose complimentary reaction to 'Masters of the Italian Line' encouraged me to have another go. Finally I would like to mention my late father John and Grandpa Jack, whose love of ships and the sea I so gratefully inherited.

To supplement the necessarily limited images and text included in the book I would like to invite you to visit my accompanying webpage at https://www.sarniawatercolours.co.uk/The-Costanzi-Quartet.html. Here you can find additional information and photographs, including deck plans.

Bibliography

Bandini, Simone & Eliseo, Maurizio, *Michelangelo e Raffaello la fine di un'epoca*, (Milan Italy: Ulrico Hoepli Editore S.p.A., 2010)

Boico, Romano, *Nicolò Costanzi artista e ingegnere "Antichità Altoadriatiche X (1976). Studi Monfalconesi e Duinati"*, (Trieste: EUT Edizioni Università di Trieste, 1976)

Braynard, Frank O & Miller, William H, *Fifty Famous Liners* (Cambridge: Patrick Stephens Limited, 1982)

Braynard, Frank O & Miller, William H, *Fifty Famous Liners 3* (New York: W.W. Norton & Company, 1987)

Dawson, Philip, *The Liner, retrospective & renaissance* (New York: W.W. Norton & Company, 2006)

Dawson, Philip & Peter, Bruce, *Ship style, modernism and modernity at sea in the 20th century* (London: Conway Maritime, 2010)

Eliseo Maurizio & Piccione Paolo, Transatlantici, *The History of the Great Italian Liners on the Atlantic*, (Genoa Italy: Tormeno Editore, 2001)

Eliseo Maurizio & Piccione Paolo, *The Costa Liners* (London: Carmania Press, 1997)

Griffiths, Denis, *Power of the Great Liners. A History of Atlantic Marine Engineering* (Sparkford: Patrick Stephens Limited 1990)

Harvey, Clive, *The Last White Empresses* (London: Carmania Press, 2004)

Kohler, Peter C, *The Lido Fleet. Italian line passenger ships & services* (Alexandria USA: Seadragon Press, 1998)

Maxtone-Graham, John, *The only way to cross* (New York: Collier Books, 1978)

Maxtone-Graham, John, *Liners to the sun* (New York:, McMillan, 1985)

Miller, William H, *Passenger liners Italian style* (London: Carmania Press, 1996)

Miller, William H, *The Last Blue Water Liners* (London: Conway Maritime Press, 1986)

Miller, William H, *Transatlantic liners* (London: David & Charles, 1981)

Miller, William H, *Great Mediterranean passenger ships* (Stroud: The History Press, 2016)

Morris, Jan, *Trieste and the meaning of nowhere* (London: Faber and Faber, 2001)

Palmer, Alan, *The Penguin dictionary of twentieth century history 1900-1978* (London: Penguin Books Ltd, 1979)

Peter, Bruce, *Knud E Hansen Design through Eight Decades* (Isle of Man: Ferry Publications, 2017)

Peter, Bruce, *Cruise Ships – A design history* (Isle of Man: Ferry Publications, 2017)

Plowman, Peter, *The Chandris Liners and Celebrity Cruises* (Australia: Rosenberg Publishing Pty Ltd, 2006)

Servello, Antonio, *Nicolo Costanzi architetto navale* (Trieste: Circolo della cultura e delle arti, 1970)

Periodicals

Meditelegraph
Sea Lines
Shipping Today and Yesterday
Ships Monthly
Syren and Shipping

Websites

www.freepatentsonline.com
www.marcellomascherini.it/?lang=en
www.midshipcentury.com
www.italianliners.com
www.sshsa.org
www.wrecksite.eu

Facebook groups

T/N Guglielmo Marconi/Galileo Galilei Viaggi Italia-Australia
SS Oceanic home lines
T/N Eugenio Costa – L'ultima vera grande nave italiana

(Photographer/source unknown)